£4·50
ge)

18/20

DOWN THE LINE TO ·BRIGHTON·

DOWN THE LINE TO ·BRIGHTON·

Muriel V. Searle

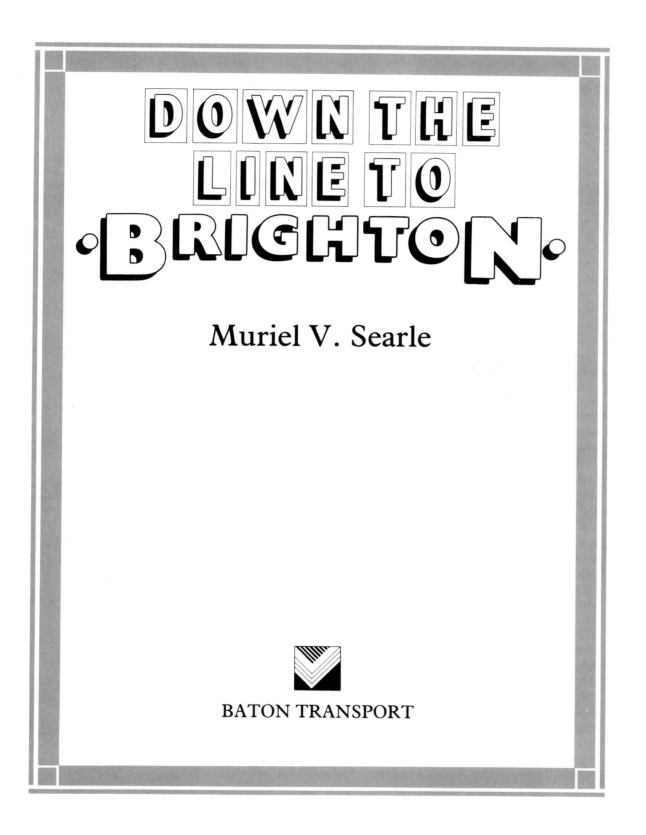

BATON TRANSPORT

Dedicated to Harold Searle:
Distant but not forgotten

In the same illustrated series:

Metro Memories by Dennis Edwards and Ron Pigram
Romance of Metro-Land by Dennis Edwards and Ron Pigram
The Golden Years of the Metropolitan Railway by Dennis Edwards and
Ron Pigram
The Final Link by Dennis Edwards and Ron Pigram
London's Underground Suburbs by Dennis Edwards and Ron Pigram
Midland Line Memories by Brian Radford
London's Underground Stations by Laurence Menear
Down the Line to Bristol by Muriel V. Searle
Down the Line to Dover by Muriel V. Searle
Down the Line to Hastings by Brian Jewell
Down the Line to Southend by Muriel V. Searle
The Settle to Carlisle by Roger Siviter
The Welsh Marches by Roger Siviter
Scottish Steam Routes by Roger Siviter

First published in 1986
BATON TRANSPORT
1 Russell Chambers
Covent Garden
London WC2E 8AA

© Muriel V. Searle 1986

ISBN 0 85936 239 6

Printed in Great Britain

Contents

Acknowledgements

The author sincerely thanks all those who helped in the compilation of this book, especially:

Mr John Barrow
Bluebell Railway
Bressingham Steam Museum
Brighton Evening Argus and *Sussex Daily News*
Brighton & Hove Gazette and *Herald*
British Rail
British Railways Board (map and pictures)
Croydon Advertiser Group of Newspapers
    ('Old & New Croydon' etc)
East Sussex County Library, Brighton Central Reference Library
    (The Erredge Collection, and pictures)
Mr John Fry
Mr George Hatcher
IPC Ltd
Illustrated London News and ILN Picture Library
Isle of Wight Steam Railway
Kent & East Sussex Railway
Mr J. Keightley
Kylin Press Ltd (*Jenny Lind*)
Mr M. Langridge
Mr D. Larkin
Lens of Sutton
Locomotive Club of Great Britain: Ken Nunn Collection
North Norfolk Railway:
Mr David Mason (including extended captions)
Orient Express Ltd
Mr T. W. L. Parker
Mr. M. A. Poupard
Mr Jack Sayers
Surrey Mirror Series
Mr P. J. Tyrrell
Ward Lock Ltd

Though the author has not quoted from *The Times*, she gratefully acknowledges it as a source of reference. A few pictures come from the author's collection of old cuttings, and their source is now unknown; it is hoped that this acknowledgement will be accepted.

Introduction

The study of railways falls into three main divisions: the technicalities of locomotives and their classes; the engineering and construction side of the lines they traversed and the stations they served; and thirdly their human and social face. The latter aspect includes their original promotion and construction, the men who guided and governed them, and the personalities and events punctuating their story.

Down the Line to Brighton concentrates on the third aspect, turning to the historical and human story of the companies which made up the London Brighton & South Coast Railway, and carried it forward into amalgamation with the Southern, and ultimately into BR.

Brighton being comparatively near to London was a town specially open to the changes railways would bring. A haunt of wealth, taste and fashion that revolved around the Prince Regent and then around the young Queen Victoria, Brighton shuddered at the very notion of the working classes ever adopting the same elegant promenades.

But Everyman did descend on Brighton directly trains made this contact possible. The gentry fled, and trade adapted itself to new custom counted in hundreds of thousands of working class small spenders, instead of only hundreds of big-house accounts from the Squares. Brighton's very soul and self changed at the moment when the first train from London rolled in.

Brighton as we and our grandparents know and knew it – the Londoners' playground by the sea – was very truly born of railways.

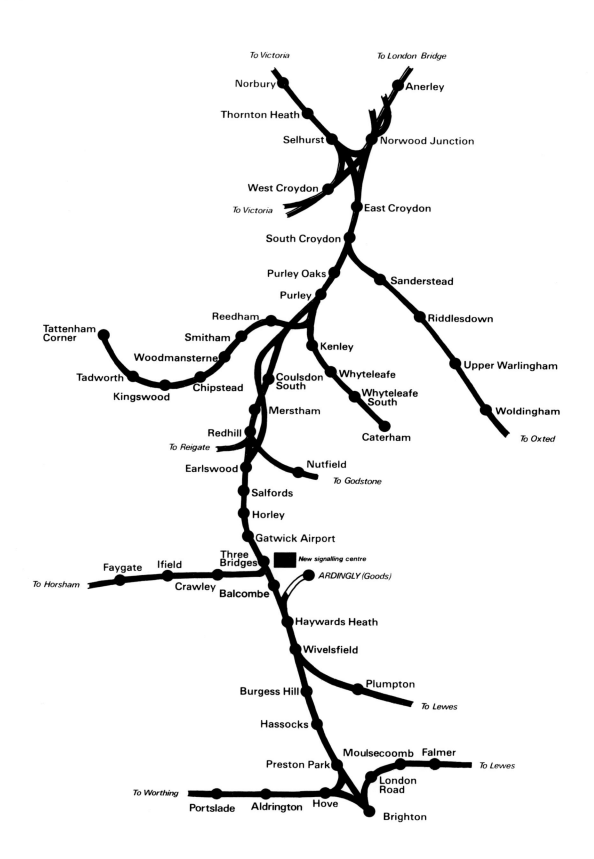

1

Into the Years of Change

'Brighthelmstone, more commonly called Brighton, now the largest and most populous town in the whole county [of Sussex], was little more than half a century ago only a small insignificant place, situated on a part of the coast but little frequented. In 1801 it contained 1,282 houses, and 7,399 inhabitants; but since that period its increase must have been astonishingly rapid, as we are assured that in 1809 there were upwards of 2,000 houses, and 12,000 settled inhabitants; and that the annual visitors, for the purpose of health or pleasure, amounted to an equal number.' So Brighton was described in 1813, during its final decades as a fashionable watering place. The notion of Everyman with his raucous family pouring down by public transport that belched smoke and steam, to drive these genteel dalliers out for ever, would have seemed absurd.

Brighton before railways

Still regal in character and appearance, Brighton had 'every possible convenience for sea bathing', including public baths for those fragile ladies who found the waves of the Channel too uncouth. At the 1801 Census it was already a centre of trade and commerce, with 3,050 people engaged in 'Trade, Manufactures, and Handicrafts', against only 94 working on the land.

Croydon, destined in time to be the main town between the coast and London, could be described in 1813 as 'a large handsome town consisting chiefly of one well built street, near a mile in length', with over 1,000 houses and 5,743 inhabitants; it was a miniature metropolis by the standards of early nineteenth-century Surrey.

The Croydon Canal was already opening up increased trade as a forerunner of railways. First proposed in 1800 and authorised by an Act the next year, it was estimated to cost about £64,100, according to its engineer Rennie. His was a name destined to become very prominent when railways instead of waterways became the way to and from Brighton.

The Grand Surrey Iron Rail Way

Already, indeed, a railway of a kind existed in Surrey, though few realised its significance. 'This road does not appear to be much used; neither is it probable that it will ever come into general use'

Locomotive Number One and antique rolling stock at the turn of the century. Class D 0-4-2T No. 1 *Sydenham* first entered service on 25th November 1873 and was followed by 124 more engines of the same class. 35 were built by Neilson & Co. and the rest at Brighton. No. 1 was scrapped in 1927.
(*LCGB/Ken Nunn Collection*)

thus a shortsighted county topographer dismissed the Grand Surrey Iron Rail Way.

By harnessing animal power to wagons whose momentum was greatly increased by the lack of resistance made possible by smooth rails instead of rutted roads, it forcefully demonstrated railways' capability in handling heavier and faster loads than was possible by road.

The Grand Surrey Iron Rail Way (or Iron Rail Road) was believed to be the first railway entered on the Statute Book, authorised by Parliament in 1801. Its best publicity came about through men betting on the speed of a horse whilst working wagons mounted on smooth rails, the beast plodding between the parallel lines. Near Merstham twelve wagons of stone, each weighing over three tons, were chained together forming a train, and one horse from a nearby timber yard was hitched on at the Fox Tavern. From there the one animal dragged this great load for six miles towards Croydon in 1hr 41mins, averaging about 4mph. He was also stopped periodically, to demonstrate how a train could start from a dead weight when on rails. The winner of the wager, flushed with success, consolidated his triumph by adding four more loaded wagons, then egged-on no fewer than fifty hefty workmen to ride on top, apparently without consigning the unfortunate horse to a state of collapse. Calculated afterwards, the total weight hauled was estimated at over fifty-five tons.

One of the earliest references to railways in Surrey and Sussex was in this context of a tramway, published on 31 December 1801: 'The modern improvement of Iron Railways is very generally adopted through the whole country . . . there is to be one of 23 miles in length in Monmouthshire . . . one in Staffordshire, where the ascent is to be 800 feet in less than four

12

miles; and it is said that the Surrey Railway is likely to be
extended through all that county, as well as in Sussex, so as to
make an easy conveyance to the coast.' On such a road, one horse
would be able to draw thirty or forty people to Brighton in six
hours; an amazing turn of speed compared with coaching,
posting, and lumbering carriers' cart.

The earliest conventional railway proposed for this area
appears to have been one mooted by William James in 1823.
Ambitiously it aimed to link London and Rochester with
Shoreham, Brighton and Portsmouth, along the South Coast.
However, the local public was not yet ready for such
developments; interest was sparse, and the scheme was dropped.

Big schemes with big names

In 1825 a Surrey, Sussex, Hampshire, Wiltshire and Somerset
Railway Company was formulated, again to link London,
Brighton and the South Coast ports, and thence up to Salisbury,
at a cost of £650,000. At that time, only the Stockton and
Darlington Railway and the Liverpool & Manchester, in the
north, existed in fact rather than as a dream on planners' drawing-
boards. A more localised Brighton and Shoreham scheme was also

13

The centrepiece of pre-railway Brighton, helping create its intensive road traffic: the Royal Pavilion in 1813, before orientalisation. (*M. V. Searle*)

considered, only to founder into oblivion. At about the same period the name of Cundy came into local notice; not initially as a railway promoter but for a proposed canal serving much the same purpose: the linking of London and the port of Shoreham. The younger John Rennie brought in his own railway proposal in 1825. The names of Charles Vignoles and Grantham Jago also entered the field.

The prospect of a future railway improved from about 1826, when a Brighton newspaper reported on an experimental atmospheric railway (prophetically for this particular line): 'A long time has elapsed since we inserted in our columns a paper relative to a mode of travelling which had been discovered, whereby the rapidity of moving to and from places of great distance from each other, might be affected in so short a time, as to remind one of some of Munchausen's flights.' The method was to propel a carriage through a specially built tunnel by atmospheric pressure, alleged to allow speeds of up to 100mph.

14

This notion was indeed revived at a later date and applied to part of what became the main Brighton railway line.

In June 1827 John Vallance the pioneer addressed a public meeting at Brighton on his idea for blowing people through a pipe from Brighton to London, but the elaborate scheme was soon abandoned and forgotten.

Road versus rail

Early nineteenth-century Brighton was so well served from London by road that many observers felt that railways were unnecessary. The rich and pretentious who had followed fashion and settled there put considerable traffic upon the main road. Forty scheduled coaches left London daily, in addition to innumerable private carriages and trade carts. Their perpetual passing wore the road's surface down and forced the authorities to keep it in better condition than most highways. On 10 January 1831, from an office in Dean's Yard, Westminster, a statement was issued concerning a 'Projected Iron Rail Road from London To Brighton', but after a meeting of landowners whose estates would be jeopardised the conclusion was adamant: 'That a railway from London to Brighton is not wanted for the purposes of commerce . . . the measure is in many respects likely to be of great injury to the community, not least to agriculture.' Solicitors and counsel were to be engaged to oppose any such Bill in Parliament.

Yet the claims of the railway developers were in fact modest: merely to carry twice as many passengers as were ferried down by road transport, which then served about 2,263 people a week, or an average of 117,676 a year. This was a tiny patronage compared with the four hundred times that number who were eventually customers of the Brighton line.

By January 1831 the Rennie brothers were involved in a London and Brighton Railway, when a directors' meeting was called to consider their engineers' estimated cost of £650,000, and the question of seeking less costly tenders for the work.

The Rennies failed to obtain a Bill when it was discovered how long-winded their construction would be, but a revised scheme appeared in 1833. In October of that year John Rennie was appointed engineer of a London-Brighton railway and began serious planning; but by then Robert Stephenson was also in the running. By November 1833 Rennie had lost about £30,000 of his own money in railway speculation.

£100 shares in a 'London and Brighton Railway with a Branch to Shoreham' were advertised in mid-1833. At about the same period the Continent was brought prospectively nearer by advertisements for a 'London, Brighton and Shoreham Railway, the Nearest Route to Paris', plans of which could be seen at the Rennie offices at Blackfriars. It foreshadowed the present Sussex (Newhaven) to Paris service in its essentials.

15

Brighton Terminus was
reconstructed in 1882 with this
splendid roof. (*M. V. Searle*)

Dreams of a Brighton line came nearer in October 1834 when a
local paper enthused: 'We understand that there is every
prospect of a revival of the project for a railway between Brighton
and London with a branch to Shoreham. A meeting of highly
respectable and influential gentlemen . . . was held at the Town
Hall, where it was, we hear, determined to take prompt steps for
the purpose of getting a Bill through Parliament . . . It was
considered that [Dover and Southampton] might supersede the
"Queen of Watering Places" if the distance between them should
be virtually lessened, as it will by a railway. The meeting
appeared to view the carrying forward of the proposed plan as a
matter of urgent necessity.'

The prime attraction of railways was speed, expected to bring
Brighton within two hours of London. Fancifully, a gentleman
could be imagined dining by the sea, seeing a London show, and
being home in Brighton for supper.

The rivals

In 1835 a town committee was appointed to consider the six
principal schemes then in circulation. They included
Stephenson's line: 53 miles via Epsom, Leatherhead, Horsham
and Shoreham; Rennie's: 47 miles through Streatham, Croydon,
Merstham, Redhill and Balcombe, much as today's route;
Cundy's: 54 miles via Epsom, Leatherhead, Dorking and
Shoreham; Gibbs': 51 miles Croydon-Ewell-Leatherhead-
Steyning-Shoreham; Palmer's: 50 miles, Croydon-Godstone-
Cuckfield; and Vignoles' line: 54 miles through Croydon,
Merstham, Horsham, Steyning and Shoreham. 1835 opened with

16

The marvellous train shed at Brighton. (*M. V. Searle*)

the three principals (Cundy, Rennie and Stephenson) each publicising a scheme he felt to be vastly superior to the others. Public meetings were held to test the opinions of leading Brighton citizens during the same summer. Also in 1835 the London & Croydon line, one of the future LBSCR's prime components, was authorised to go ahead, taking rails well on the way towards Brighton.

Promoters' advertisements multiplied for the rival routes, such as those for 'The London and Brighton Rail-Road through Epsom, Leatherhead, Dorking, Horsham and Shoreham; Capital One Million in Ten Thousand Shares of One Hundred Pounds'. Or, again, 'London and Brighton Railway with a Branch to Shoreham' with G. and J. Rennie as engineers. The South Eastern Railway advertised its own encroachment into Brighton through Oxted and Lindfield and added: 'This is not only the shortest and most direct practicable line to Brighton, but also has the advantage, for the first twenty miles out of London, of a joint communication with the counties of Sussex and Kent, offering thereby a double source of profit [to shareholders] for that part . . . The Survey has been completed and the Parliamentary Notices will be given in due time.' Brighton, so famous and prosperous, was an inevitable magnet to the railway developer, inviting those who called themselves businessmen to invest at all costs somewhere among the competing schemes.

Rigours of the railway: 19th century. (*Leisure Hour*)

Others, however, were not so sure. Coach services were excellent, a mere 4½ hours' run from the Golden Cross in London. And 'who wanted to go to Brighton, anyway?' said the more sarcastic among journalists.

Suspicion about railway speeds compared with those of horses increased after the first accidents occurred elsewhere, notably one causing loss of life upon the new 'toy' from Liverpool to

17

Manchester, and another incident upon 'the new tomfoolery to Greenwich'.

Nothing seemed more ridiculous to one famous journal than a Greenwich railroad; yet the Greenwich Railway did open, in 1836, and become an integral part (over one of its sections) for the Brighton service of the future.

'These newfangled absurdities', as one debunker called railways, appeared throughout the land, and by 1835 financial returns could be compared for various real or proposed schemes, including the London & Brighton: 30,000 shares at £20 (capital £600,000); the London & Greenwich: 20,000 shares of £20 (£400,000); the London & Croydon: 8,000 shares of £50 (£400,000); and the London to Shoreham & Brighton: 18,000 £50 shares (£900,000). Big money was in the air whenever and wherever railways were contemplated, beyond the understanding of a navvy employed to work on them for £1 a week, or less.

The 'Direct London & Brighton Railway with a Branch to Shoreham' was advertised in February 1836 as 'the shortest and the direct one', when rumours of its premature abandonment were vigorously denied. Rennie's directors asserted that it would save nine miles on the distance, had easy curves and gradients and would save time and fares by its short mileage, and was comparatively cheap to acquire, and about £4,500 a year could be saved in maintenance – again because of shorter mileage. Better still, the directors could boast of a reduction in building costs of no less than £750,000 'by adopting the Croydon and Greenwich line as the London terminus'. The London and Greenwich Railway from Spa Road at Bermondsey to Deptford opened a few days after this statement was issued, and the Londonward section on 14 December. The 'new tomfoolery to Greenwich' was to prove very useful to the emergent Brighton line.

Neck and neck

Rennie and Stephenson were both pushing schemes into the Commons, but gradually Rennie drew ahead, partly on his claim that the shortest route and shortest timings were the most logical, especially as the line was likely to be exceptionally heavily geared to passengers and far less to freight; a balance which remained constant throughout its history.

Cundy's prime selling point was a 'Brighton Railway Without a Tunnel'. Some misconception arising on Cundy's relationship with Parliament prompted him to publish a letter from the Clerk of the Committee of the House of Commons of 24 March 1836: 'I am desired by the Committee upon the London & Brighton Railroads Bills, to inform you that they have come to the following resolution: That Mr Cundy be allowed to put in his line, and upon so doing be heard by Council in support thereof.' The scheme was generally advertised as 'Brighton Railway (Without Tunnels)', as in a typical retort to the Stephenson

The headcode indicates that the train is from Victoria to Stoats Nest, later called Coulsdon North, and quite recently closed. The locomotive is Class A1 0-6-0T No. 662 and in Stroudley's day it was named *Martello* and numbered 62 when built in October 1875 at Brighton. It became British Railways No. 32662 and was withdrawn in December 1963 having run 1½ million miles. The locomotive was then purchased by Butlins and installed at the Heads of Ayr holiday camp. In the early 1970s it was transferred to Bressingham gardens in Norfolk.

(LCGB/Ken Nunn Collection)

camp: 'It may be stated with confidence, that the general effect of the evidence given in support of Mr Stephenson's line, is to show the advantages of Mr Cundy's line, from which it is admitted Mr Stephenson has generally adopted his projected line.' Share certificates in the Line Without a Tunnel were offered from 14 April 1836 from a London office in New Bond Street.

The cost of beginning

The expenses of railway planning could be high, particularly for compensating farmers and property owners whose fields a line must cross, and businesses which got in the way of progress, not to mention rival forms of transport traversing the same countryside. Thus the Croydon Canal's owners were awarded £40,250 for selling out, this to include 'the canal, reservoirs, buildings, lands attached and detached, and other property belonging to the Canal company'.

A permanent changeover of Brighton from genteel watering place to noisy popular resort was now seen to be inescapable. Once given railways, said a contemporary weekly journal, Cockneys would over-run the place, squawking with excitement at seeing something previously reserved for the rich who were able to travel – the sea. How quickly they realised the benefit of 'Doctor Brighton' was demonstrated in women like the writer's great-grandmother, whose daughters were told to take their

One of the 35 D class tanks built by Neilson & Co. in November 1881. No. 251 *Singleton* was renumbered B251 by the Southern Railway and scrapped in 1926. The guard is well protected by the bulge in his front compartment. Through the windows he can observe signals and communicate with the footplate crew, as well as checking the train for open doors upon leaving a station.
(*LCGB/Ken Nunn Collection*)

infants to a hilltop fifty miles north, at Bromley in Kent, in the belief that Brighton Breezes came there straight across country to do them good.

Money pours into railway schemes

It was popularly rumoured that nearly a million pounds were to be subscribed to Cundy's project, one of the main contenders for award of a Brighton development. Cundy's big advantage was a low level route, which needed less elaborate cuttings and tunnels and had none of those particularly high embankments considered dangerous since the recent upset of 120 passengers on the Liverpool & Manchester Railway. Above all, it lacked tunnels; not even one plunge underground was envisaged, hence the constant press advertisements identifying it to the public as the line 'Without A Tunnel'.

Rumour so plagued the railway-kings that frequent denials had to be issued, such as this example of 8 May 1836: 'LONDON SHOREHAM AND BRIGHTON RAILWAY WITHOUT A TUNNEL: A report being still industriously circulated that Mr Cundy has sold his line to certain interested parties [who, doubtless would be but too happy to purchase], the Provisional Committee of this undertaking only notice the report for the purpose of informing the Shareholders that . . . ample proof will be readily afforded them that their interests have been legally secured in the most complete manner.'

20

On 31 May 1836 a Commons Committee sitting considered all three main Brighton proposals (Cundy, Rennie and Stephenson) and prepared to report. The Line Without A Tunnel stood out to such advantage (admitted to exist by Rennie's lawyers and not questioned by Stephenson's Counsel) that a favourable report was expected. Cundy's camp were therefore incensed by a newspaper advertisement alleging that only two instead of three lines were under scrutiny, putting out their own counter-announcement that they were still very much in the field.

Stephenson's rival scheme, despite taking a longer route, could bring patrons into Brighton six minutes earlier than by Rennie's route: to quote a contemporary adage, adopted by the railway world: 'The furthest way round is the nearest way home.' Others preferred the truism about the shortest distance being a straight line; Victorian speech was so full of adages and truisms that they could be twisted to mean two quite different things.

Objections to Stephenson's ideas centred on railways' despoilation of 'ornamental scenery'. To save money, Rennie proposed not to landscape his cuttings but to leave them almost sheer, unsightly and vulnerable to frost erosion. Passengers would endure up to four miles of dingy tunnels and fourteen miles of dark cuttings. Additionally, Rennie's tight curves were considered dangerous, and precluded any real turn of speed. Stephenson's line at that time seemed to have the advantages, and Rennie's most of the bad points, as newspaper reports, denials and counter-denials batted the subject back and forth.

While businessmen in the railway world were pouring out their fine descriptive eulogies of railways, the person who mattered most – Everyman, John Citizen, or Mr Brighton – was as cut off as ever from the wider world. He could watch line surveyors at work as he trundled past by the road transport of countless centuries past, but was no nearer to actually riding on a train than he was a decade before.

Pamphleteering was still at its peak as a lettered men's diversion, and railways did not escape. One author forcibly put the current situation back in debate with *Statements and Reflections on the Brighton Railroad, without a Tunnel* in June 1836; he was exhaustive and unflattering in his analysis of trains and all connected with them.

A heated subject produced a heated press when the early nineteenth-century took up its pen.

The planners continued to plan; the gentry to cringe before the prospect of the unlettered masses invading their elegant town; the clergy to denounce iron horses as inventions of the Devil, breathing out the black smoke of Hades; and more far-sighted observers to look forward cautiously to the imminent new age.

2

The Royal Assent

In June 1836, three proposed lines were before Parliamentary Committees: Rennie's, Stephenson's and Cundy's. Briefly compared, their statistics ran: *Rennie* – including Shoreham section: 55½ miles, 5 tunnels, 22 'undulating inclined planes', one 10-ton engine being able to take 10 carriages of 180 passengers from London to Brighton in 2hr 51min, and freight at 2s 6d (12½p) a ton; *Stephenson* – 56 miles 51 chains, only 4 tunnels, 22 undulating planes, proposed speed 16½–30mph, an 8-ton engine to take 10 coaches or 20 tons of freight in 2hr 35½min; and *Cundy* – 54 miles 60 chains, with no tunnels, and only 6 inclined planes. A 7-ton engine was to draw the same number of coaches in 2hr 7min for 2s 2d (10½p) per ton or per passenger; with only eight-on, London and Brighton could be linked in 1hr 37min. In this context one passenger equalled one ton of goods.

Committees and more committees

In July the various proposals were before the Lords, with Stephenson now favourite, and Cundy's 'direct line without tunnels' a close second. Geographically the possible ways into Brighton were very varied, ranging from valley meanderings to bold slashings of the Downs, the latter inevitably involving tunnels. Public suspicion of tunnels was deep, and their scope for annihilating trains and passengers underground was given full voice.

To quote one of many reports: 'The cause of the Brighton Railway Without A Tunnel has been fairly heard in the House of Lords . . . it has been a fair stand-up fight and no favour . . . Dr Thompson and several others, most eminent in the profession, gave their opinion . . . so decidedly against tunnels that we are confident that all the Peers . . . will vote for a postponement of the question till next year, as there is no tunnel on a railroad for passengers yet open, in order to try the practical effect of tunnels.'

Fear of the unknown, or the little known, was the bane of every developer whose visions were of speed and progress.

Medical men as well as laymen had their doubts as to the effects of speed and steam on human constitutions, particularly of the delicate female species.

The tunnel question thus was debated on medical as well as practical grounds. In August 1836 Sir Anthony Carlisle, Vice

VIEW OF BRIGHTON, FROM ROSE HILL NORTH

THE BRIGHTON RAILROAD

QUADRILLES,

AND

Pavilion Waltz,

Composed for the Pianoforte

& DEDICATED TO THE

VISITORS OF BRIGHTON,

BY

FREDk WRIGHT.

Ent. Sta. Hall

M&N Hanhart lith. Printer, 64 Charlotte St Rathbone Pl.

Published by

WRIGHT & SONS,

MUSIC SELLERS TO THE QUEEN & MUSICAL INSTRUMENT DEALERS,

ROYAL COLONADE, BRIGHTON.

Opening day of the Shoreham
section on 11 May 1840:
crowds admire the first trains.
(*Brighton Reference Library*)

President of the College of Surgeons, thundered a whole column
of objections to the Press; to cite but a few: 'The difference in
temperature in tunnels will expose persons in health to the
common affection notoriously termed catching cold, the source
of other disorders . . . On persons of weak constitution, or who
are invalids, passing through a tunnel will cause more striking
and more remarkable effects . . . I would not permit one of my
patients to go to Brighton by a railway that had a tunnel in it . . .
Certainly [I] would dissuade any patient from subjecting himself
to such perils . . . I say that in the transit of only one minute he is
in peril, and I would not so expose myself.'

Dr James Johnson, a physician to His Majesty, repeated these
dire prognostications: 'The reverberation would be tremendous
with a locomotive engine, and give a very great shock to delicate
people . . . [I] would not send persons liable to affections in the
heart or head through those tunnels . . . Would not send a
delicate lady by a railroad of this sort, nor a lady in a state of
pregnancy.' Yet surely no train would have exceeded the jolting,
lurching, swaying, travel-sickening motion of a stage coach on an
unmade road, to which these same people were accustomed.

The end of 1836

In August 1836 a 'South Eastern Brighton, Lewes and
Newhaven Railway, Joining the South Eastern Railway Near
Oxted', was still in the debate, ruled by a bevy of two dozen
committee-men of wealth and power. It was described as having
a terminus in Brighton at the Great Northern Entrance, a point

24

allegedly approved by local inhabitants for its convenience. Capital at 30 August was £1,100,000 in £50 shares, with W. Cubitt as consulting engineer and W. A. Provis as engineer. Shares were again offered in the rival London & Brighton Railway Without a Tunnel on 2 September, to be had on surrender of the old shares.

On 3 December it could be announced that for yet another scheme, the Direct London & Brighton Railway, 'plans, sections and books of reference of the Direct Line as improved, and its proposed branches' had been 'duly deposited with the respective Clerks of the Peace'.

The year of decision

1837 brought an end to all these schemes and counter-schemes, giving Brighton the prospect of action, instead of the speechifying by so many different promoters that the public was merely bewildered instead of excited by the prospect of being propelled into the railway age. In the popular press the contenders were narrowed again to Stephenson, Rennie, and Cundy. A resolution was successfully eased through the Commons Committee in April, 'that the termini of Stephenson's line of railway, both at London and Brighton, are inconvenient to the public, that the line is circuitous and several miles longer than others now under consideration'. The field was rapidly narrowing.

In an amalgamation of interests the Direct Brighton and the South Eastern Brighton Railway Company joined forces instead of continuing to bicker.

Finally, a Government Engineer was appointed to scrutinise the main remaining schemes and report in favour of one of them. Almost certainly the most direct line would win. Rennie was favoured, and on 15 July 1837 the Brighton Railway of the future received the Royal Assent to its enabling Act. The London & Brighton and the South Eastern were to take a common route over the final miles into London.

Brighton (as well as Newhaven) was to be given consideration as a port, interlinked by trains to the Continent when Europe, too, went over to rail transport. In September 1838 the French Government steamer *Papin* brought in the Mayor of Dieppe and an official party of enthusiasts, who were pledged to build a railway from Dieppe to Paris, to sample for themselves the possible timings of the route. This experimental voyage took 8hr 23min, about double today's time, but it was believed possible to reduce this journey to about six hours at sea. On this assumption, the total London-Paris link via Brighton should be achieved in 'the almost incredibly short space of twelve hours', opening up a 'new era of prosperity' to Brighton in the role of inter-Continental port.

Railway building operations began in earnest late in 1837, with the line marked out from the prospective terminus in Church

Street under the supervision of Rennie and his colleague Rastrick. The total scheme was divided for easy management into three sections, each under a resident engineer. Even in these early days a subdivision of the human species, which is the plague of railways today, made his first appearance in Brighton: the vandal on the line. It was reported that 'Some mischievous or malignant persons have taken it into their heads to destroy some of the marks laid down in the Direct-Line of railway. The Company have offered a reward for the discovery of the offenders.'

Progress into the railway age

A progress report was expected to be presented by Rennie and Rastrick in November 1837, to dispel any remaining doubts that this was 'the only line of railroad which can be carried into effect consistently with the interests of Brighton'.

Subscribers were told that a tunnel at Merstham had been substituted for open cuttings and the tunnels at Balcombe and Clayton had been lengthened. Total cuttings had been reduced from 9,251,000 cubic yards of excavated earthworks, down to only 5,867,000 cubic yards.

Sir John Rennie and John Urpeth Rastrick were now joint engineers of the London & Brighton Railway, and the latter was appointed to make further working surveys for both Brighton and Shoreham areas. By then the cost of the two lines, including stations and 'every contingency', was estimated at £920,000: a vast sum for the average man working on the line to grasp, when his week's hard toil brought in just £1, or even less. With the costs of acquiring land, the total rose to £1,120,000 but, once operational, the directors expected to reap a good £305,000 a year.

Compensation ran away with tens of thousands of pounds and caused much contention, as is clear from a case heard at Brighton Town Hall in 1838 to settle payment to Thomas Reed Kemp for fifteen acres. Examination of builders' witnesses supporting the railway's claim to Kemp's property took a whole day, the estimated value of the property being up to £44,000. Conversely, Kemp's agent cited the £3 to £4 per foot of frontage obtainable on land for housing instead of railway lines, and claimed an additional £10,000 for devaluation to property cut apart by the line running across it.

In 1838 the first stone was laid for an observatory on Clayton Hill, under which Clayton Tunnel would run. It hammered home to passing coach drivers on the nearby road the inescapable truth that horse travel was doomed, and with it their livelihood.

Swearing like a navvy

'Swearing like a navvy' went into colloquial speech as these rowdy uncouth labourers flooded the countryside to hammer and crash,

LONDON and BRIGHTON RAILWAY.—This Railway will be opened on TUESDAY next, 21st September, throughout from London to Brighton, for the conveyance of passengers, parcels, private carriages, and horses.

DOWN TRAINS from LONDON DAILY, except Sundays.—Mixed Train at ¾ past 9 a.m.; First Class Train at ¾ past 10 a.m.; Mixed Train at ¾ past 1 p.m.; Mixed Train at ¾ past 2 p.m.; First Class Train at ¾ past 3 p.m.; Express Train at ¾ past 4 p.m.; Mixed Train to Croydon only at 7 p.m.

The Mixed Trains will arrive at Brighton in two hours and a half, the First Class Trains in two hours, and the Express Train in one hour and three quarters.

SUNDAY TRAINS down from London—Mixed Trains, at 8 a.m., ¾ past 10 a.m., and 7 p.m.; and a Mixed Train to Croydon only at 10 p.m.

UP TRAINS from BRIGHTON DAILY, except Sundays—Mixed Train at ¾ past 6 a.m.; Express Train at ¼ past 8 a.m.; First Class Train at ¾ past 10 a.m.; Mixed Train at ¾ past 11 a.m.; First Class Train at ¼ past 2 p.m.; Mixed Train at 4 p.m; and a Mixed Train from Croydon only at ¾ past 2 p.m.

SUNDAY TRAINS up from Brighton—Mixed Trains at ¾ past 7 a.m., at 4 p.m., and at 7 p.m.; and an up Train mixed from Croydon only at 7 a.m.

Fares to and from London and Brighton—First Class Carriages, 14s. 6d.; Second Class, 9s. 6d.; Children in Second Class, 6s. 6d.

Fares to Croydon—First Class, 2s.; Second Class, 1s. 6d.

N.B.—No Passenger will be conveyed from London to New Cross, or New Cross to London.

The Express Train will stop nowhere on the Line to take up or set down Passengers.—The First Class Train will stop only at Croydon, Red Hill, Three Bridges, and Hayward's Heath.

The Mixed Trains only consist of First and Second Class Carriages, and will stop at every station on the Line.

Children under 10 years of age, in First Class Carriages, will be charged Second Class Fare. No charge made for infants in arms.

Bills containing all particulars as to the conveyance of carriages, horses, dogs, luggage, and parcels, together with information as to omnibuses, post horses, &c., may be had on application at the Offices of the Company, 10, Angel court, Throgmorton-street, or at the following Booking offices:—Griffins, and Green Man and Still, Oxford-street; Hatchett's, Piccadilly, and 41 Regent-circus, Spread Eagle, ditto; Golden Cross, Charing-cross; George and Blue Boar, Holborn; Old Bull, Holborn; White Horse, Fetter-lane; Cross Keys, Wood-street; and the Spread Eagle, Gracechurch-street.

By order,

THOMAS WOOD, Secretary.

17th Sept., 1841.

blaspheme and brawl, insult farmers' wives and ogle their daughters, in a manner never before seen in peaceful Sussex. It was said that once the line was finished it would bring a further wave of rabble who would likewise care nothing for the Queen of Watering Places except as a noisy amusement ground: 'A class of persons objectionable to the visitors of rank and fashion who are in the habit of resorting hither, and who will not be disposed to mix with them.'

Still more gangs of navvies were drafted in as the works came alive; hard-drinking, hard-swearing, and hard-womanising. We read how in 1838 a Portslade gentleman brought to the local magistrates' notice the behaviour of a gang prevented from working by teeming rain; temporarily free, they spent a whole day in 'drunkenness and rioting to the great annoyance of the peaceable inhabitants of Portslade'. The sole village bobby was no match for nearly two hundred uncouth drunks.

Rennie's London & Brighton Railway Company reported after its first General Meeting on the actual layout of the line to run from

London Bridge over part of the Greenwich and Croydon railways, then past Merstham and Reigate, Horley, Balcombe and Cuckfield through Clayton, and terminating at Church Street. 26,172 shares were registered as at 18 January 1838, with 7,901 more applied for. It was then estimated that construction would take three years. The nature of the traffic was summed up exactly as it was to be throughout the line's life: primarily a passenger railway with far fewer freight movements than elsewhere. Passengers were the lifeblood of the coaching trade; now they would be the lifeblood of the railway that would banish coaching.

The coming of tunnels

In March 1838 shafts for the main tunnels were sunk, including Clayton which was considered to be a difficult working due to seepage of water. As well as that on Clayton Hill above the new tunnel, observatories were built commanding the Balcombe and Merstham sections of the line, each enclosing 'an apparatus that secures the direction of the tunnels, and during progress of the work the whole line is under the observation of the three resident engineers'.

Ground was first broken on 12 July 1838 in the deepest part of the big cutting north of Merstham Tunnel.

Clayton Hill observatory was operational by July and the actual shafts were begun. The Shoreham branch was expected to be started on 22 July, starting with an embankment through Goldstone Bottom, working towards Brighton. The only temporary setback was a fall in share values, after the failure of a speculator holding excessive numbers who then forced them onto the market. By August the *Brighton Gazette* could report rapid progress; Clayton Hill observatory was finished and the Shoreham branch was about to be begun in earnest.

Stagecoaches still trundled through Sussex, but instead of gazing at farmland scenery, passengers stared in awe and curiosity at the railway works constantly coming into view. They saw sweating gangs labouring with earth and stone, straining horses, machinery belching steam, and all the other trappings of the iron horse, which was soon to replace the four-legged horse.

3

Five Thousand Men and Fifty Horses

Suddenly, the benefit of railways became more apparent, particularly in the shape of money. It was realised that when people flocked down to Brighton in tens of thousands instead of mere hundreds, the local trade would prosper. Thus a local paper changed its tune: 'Many were of the opinion that a railroad to Brighton would inundate the town with the scum of the Metropolis, and that it would eventually destroy its character as a place of fashionable resort; but that idea is fast subsiding, and instead of having the London disreputables, we expect to be numerously visited by respectable tradesmen and merchants.' Or to give another contemporary opinion: 'Half the population of London will be constantly travelling to the seashore, and many a Cockney who never saw the broad ocean before, will then feast his eyes on the wonders of the mighty deep. The benefits of railroads will then be duly appreciated.'

The cost of living was expected to be reduced once railways came, bringing in cheap food and goods from London, and destroying local monopolies' tendency to cash-in on shortages.

On 14 March 1839 the railway directors met to consider tenders for three main contracts. Firstly, at Patcham, to 'make and maintain the railway with the excavations, embankments, brickwork, masonry, bridges, culverts, drains, fences, gates, lodges and other works complete'. Secondly a Preston contract for works between Field Number Twenty in Patcham parish and the road from the Dairy House to New England Farm; and thirdly a section from that Farm to Trafalgar Street, including 'the forming and levelling of the station at Brighton'.

Compensation to landowners

The Kemp compensation case was duly settled at £25,000, giving some parties a sense of dissatisfaction that he had not bargained harder for twice that sum. This come-down in price was considered base ingratitude by the railway company towards a citizen who had been more cooperative than most. Other compensation cases included those of a Mrs Raven, who wanted £1,500 for one acre at Croydon (reduced by a jury to £600); that of Sir Charles Blunt also of Croydon, claiming three thousand guineas but awarded only £1,423.15s; and Messrs Fisher who asked £725.16s for seven acres at Coulsdon, again reduced by jury to only £447.12s.

Victorian decoration remaining at East Croydon. (*M. V. Searle*)

The first permanent rail was laid on 4 February 1839 at Hassocks Gate by the Clerk to the Brighton Board of Guardians.

Contemporary reports frequently mentioned the Brighton Railroad rather than railway, a term now generally considered an Americanism. Under this heading came a report of 23 April 1839 on works in the New England area. With two hundred men preparing the Trafalgar Street station site, these excavations were being termed 'stupendous'. At The Wick, towards Shoreham, earth and chalk were gouged out, with a contractor's engine almost perpetually in steam between there and Southwick. Also in April 1839 a new engine, the *Shoreham*, arrived. It was hauled into Brighton by fourteen horses on a Tuesday evening, and dragged on to Portslade next morning and placed onto the rails. Thereafter she worked with the smaller 2-2-2 *Brighton*. *Shoreham* distinguished herself by once hauling 27 loaded wagons at a speed of 20mph. Other engines soon joined these two, likewise named after lineside sites: *Coulsdon, Kingston*, and *Merstham*.

The line had its share of Dismal Jimmies, prophesying the collapse of cuttings, or trains entombed in tunnels; the 'dropsical' state of the Balcombe and Clayton hills was eagerly seized upon, and the terrain reckoned by some critics to be so formidable that the developers would retreat.

Exertions redoubled on the Shoreham part, but opening day was further delayed as torrential rain hindered completion of the last three miles. A brief opening ceremony was staged in May 1839, but work resumed almost immediately further east, on the cuttings near Hove, and on a tunnel due to be opened by July. In May the foundation stone of the New England viaduct was laid with a display of Masonic ceremony staged by the Royal Clarence

The old but still serviceable long platform ramps at East Croydon date from 1898 when the New and East Croydon stations were rebuilt into one station. (*M. V. Searle*)

Lodge of Freemasons. The Masons marched to the site from the Old Ship Hotel with their flags, banners and craft symbols, and a Bible borne on a red velvet cushion. This was said to be the only turn-out of the Brighton Freemasons in such style. The admiring crowds supposedly numbered ten thousand people.

Strikes proved to be a well-established custom, even as early as 1839, including a down-tools by men at the Brighton end of the Shoreham section, vaguely reported as 'on account of some dispute'.

Gapers and gawpers watching men at work were, likewise, nothing new. Hundreds visited this section daily, jostling and crowding for the thrill of riding to Southwick on the contractor's engine. Somehow, somebody was always able to abandon his own work to stare at other people's labours.

As the first full opening day approached, of the London & Croydon Railway, special trains were run for directors and shareholders to view the works. London & Brighton Railway directors, with deputations from the Greenwich Railway, were taken in two special trains early in June 1839 to see the new stations to Croydon, completing the run in under half-an-hour; among them were the Lord Mayor and Lady Mayoress of London, many MPs, and scores of expensively-gowned ladies. New Cross was inspected, particularly its massive octagonal engine house for sixteen locomotives, filled with light from a lofty cupola instead of the gloom of the railway-age. The party's

The old passenger walkways down to the East Croydon platforms. (*M. V. Searle*)

attention was drawn to an incline of two miles, and some bridges of 'peculiar' design. After arrival at Croydon the distinguished company was ferried to the London Tavern for a formal lunch with the Coldstream Guards' band in attendance.

Because patriotism demanded that royalty should somehow be linked with railway affairs, the opening of the Croydon Railway, the first leg of the total London-Brighton journey, was made to coincide with Her Majesty's birthday. The 11am celebration train of twelve carriages was appropriately hauled by the new engine *Victoria*. The full public opening came on 5 July 1839, trains using in part the Greenwich Railway's tracks as a London exit, at a toll of 3d (1p) a passenger. The first train out, at 8.30am, was packed with excited passengers, each eager to boast for life of having ridden on the London & Croydon Railway on its official opening day.

The price of land

Differences with landowners continued to punctuate development, the usual procedure being for the owner to hold out for a high price until he was beaten down to something more realistic. Wrangling over some disputed acres at Southwick brought work temporarily to a standstill. Meanwhile the new Croydon section settled down to business, though not always to the satisfaction of its patrons. Advertisements for the trains lured people off the roads to marvel at reaching Norwood from London (Tooley Street) at almost every hour of the day, but truth was well divorced from copy-writers' fiction. Once landed at Jolly Sailor station

32

Historic inscribed glass surviving today. (*M. V. Searle*)

(afterwards Norwood or Norwood Junction), passengers found themselves two miles from Norwood proper, and likewise from the popular pleasance of Beulah Spa, a public garden anticipating the Crystal Palace with its balloon ascents, outdoor dancing, pageants and fireworks. Far from being 'centrical' to Norwood, Jolly Sailor was but the start of a long uphill slog, making the total journey slower than by horse-drawn coach.

Meetings and resolutions

Early history was regularly charted by shareholders' and directors' meetings, into which the spirit of Victorian philanthropy somehow managed to intrude itself; as in July 1839 when at a half-yearly general meeting of the emergent London & Brighton Railway it was resolved that 'a sum not exceeding £100 be presented annually to the two applications made on behalf of the Church Pastoral Aid Society'. The March 1840 meeting of London & Croydon proprietors was told that all expenses had been met to date, and that tolls due to the Greenwich Railway for using a short section of its Londonward tracks had been duly paid.

The London & Brighton Railway also paid a £5,000 share in enlarging London Bridge station to accommodate the expected increased traffic.

On 1 May 1840 the public was informed that the Shoreham branch of the London & Brighton Railway was now open to seven trains daily, at 9 and 11am, and at 1, 3, 5, 7, and 9pm, and from Shoreham two-hourly at 8, 10, and 12am; 2, 4, 6, and 8pm.

Rastrick's Ouse Valley Viaduct in 1983. The stains on the brickwork are caused by rainwater washing the lime out of the mortar. The true art of the bricklayers of the 1840s can be seen best from inside the arches of the viaduct. One of the 'Cathedrals of Industry'. (*D. J. Mason*)

The main opening came on 11 May, but some authorities preferred that the Shoreham branch actually opened on 26 May 1840, at 5½ miles long.

Five return services ran on Sundays, and fares were fixed at one shilling (5p) First Class; ninepence (4½p) Second; and sixpence (2½p) Third. The ultimate luxury was 'the coupé of the First Class Carriage' at a princely 1s 4d (6½p). The booking offices closed sharply at departure times, allowing for no latecomers. An initial cost of £150,000 was quickly recovered, and in the first three months an average of 5,000 people were carried weekly.

By July 1840 the London & Brighton Railway engineers felt

The LBSCR completely rebuilt Brighton station in 1882/3 and in so doing obscured the classical Italianate frontage of David Mocatta with a steel and glass canopy. In 1979 and 1980 new offices were opened on the premises and the rebuilt frontage now vaguely resembles the original outline.
(*M. V. Searle*)

confident of opening down to Hooley Lane, six miles south of the Croydon Railway, within three months.

The massive Ouse Viaduct near Haywards Heath, the line's most spectacular engineering feat, was subjected to the customary finishing-off ceremony when in December 1840 the final arch was keyed by Maude, the engineer of the line's middle section. Visitors drove in from Brighton and Lewes to cheer at the appropriate moment. The statistics given by the *Brighton Gazette* were undeniably impressive: 'The viaduct consists of two abutments and 37 semicircular arches, of a 40-foot span, and varying in height from 48 to 96 feet. The entire length of the viaduct is 1,475 feet, or rather more than a quarter of a mile, and the width of the railway is 28 feet. Upwards of 11,300,000 bricks, made from the soil of the neighbourhood, have been used in the structure, independently of about 480,000 feet of masonry in the foundations and elsewhere . . . This stupendous undertaking has been completed in about 18 months.'

At the peak of the Brighton Railway building works over 5,000 men and 50 horses were employed, in addition to steam driven machinery. The cost was estimated at about £23,376 a mile but, rapid increases in cost being nothing new, the real figure rose to £37,568, up by 60%, which even today's inflation-conscious world would find hard to accept. The excuses given were that 'the works were unusually heavy, with numerous and difficult bridges and

35

viaducts, long and costly tunnels, and earthworks of more than common magnitude'.

First inspections

A line inspection was made in March 1841, using one locomotive and one carriage sent out from London Bridge to Hooley Lane, sixteen miles south. The committee members then walked through Merstham tunnel; joined another train for Earlswood Common; walked another section and then were taken to Balcombe tunnel to walk through that unfinished cavern to Kemp's Farm. The keying of the last part of Clayton tunnel provoked Victorian pomp and pride, with some two hundred spectators taken out by an elaborately decorated train of seven coaches, to see the last brick put into place with a special trowel, by Statham, the resident engineer of that section of track.

The London & Brighton Railway opened from Croydon (Norwood) through to Haywards Heath on 12 July 1841, with just two months still to go before full completion. The first public services comprised four 'up' and four 'down' trains daily via Croydon, Merstham and Horley. Agreement was reached with Brighton's coach proprietors for conveying passengers the rest of the way; an arrangement doomed to result in chaos, confusion and contention. This last leg to Brighton was made by horsedrawn coach, lengthening the total journey to four hours, no better than taking coach all the way under power of the hoofed instead of the iron horse.

Because coach accommodation was limited, places must be booked the previous day, but still scuffles broke out as too many passengers with luggage battled to cram themselves into too few seats. A First Class ticket ensured no preferential treatment, and a wealthy gentleman might well be forced onto the outside rooftop seats whilst Second Class people were inside. If he did get inside, his luggage could be left behind at Haywards Heath, or put onto a different vehicle. A surcharge of 8s (40p) did not ensure against being left behind, and nobody bothered about inspecting tickets which were made out for inside or outside coach seats, nor did the company number them to ensure fairness.

From July 1841 the first daily train left London at 9.30am for Croydon (10am), Godstone Road (10.10), Stoat's Nest (10.14), Merstham (10.30) and on towards Balcombe (11.16) and Haywards Heath, arriving there at 11.30am. Only three more trains followed, at 11.30am; 1.30 and 5pm; plus a 9pm to Croydon only. At some intermediate stations, trains only stopped on specific request. Fares from London to Croydon were 2s (10p) First Class; 1s 6d (7½p) Second; to Godstone Road 2s 6d (12½p) and 2s (10p); to Balcombe 8s 6d (42½p) or 6s 6d (32½p); and to Brighton (including the horse-coach) 15s (75p) and 11s (55p); expensive when set against comtemporary incomes. Horses and

carriages were also conveyed from Croydon and Haywards Heath, on attached flat trucks which anticipated today's motorail. Charges ranged from £1.1s (£1.05) down to 2s 2d (11p) for a four-wheeled or two-wheeled carriage, with each owner's one, two or three horses conveyed. Passengers staying aboard their own carriages paid at Second Class rail fare. Post-horses could be arranged at Haywards Heath and Croydon to take private vehicles forward to their destinations.

During the first operational week to Haywards Heath, 2,483 passengers paid total fares of £925. 5s. 9d (925.29½).

Stranded

Passengers were often delayed at Haywards Heath for an hour because of far too few connecting coaches; the worst such incident left forty people behind for three hours, without any immediate prospect of reaching Brighton. Their only amusement meanwhile was to loudly criticise the railway directors' morals in charging the fare to Brighton and leaving their stranded customers several miles inland. Some even temporarily deserted trains, and returned to coaching all the way.

Nor were the trains themselves above reproach; the best that could be said was that 'the original Third Class carriages were of the poorest description, very much resembling . . . cattle trucks'. Cows, indeed, fared better, with roofs over them; humans were open to wind, weather and coal smuts in open trucks, sometimes without seats, and with only an iron rail to hold, putting up their umbrellas against flying ash and cinders to save themselves being burned.

More and more men found employment on the new line, and in July 1841 no fewer than three hundred extra navvies were engaged.

Any mishap swept the neighbourhood with rumour, until a major disaster was bandied from mouth to mouth, as in September just before the final opening day, when a train failed to reach its destination. An hour elapsed, during which tales of multiple casualties circulated. The truth was that one engine with one single carriage containing an inspector and his wife had been sent out to deliver to railway policemen at wayside stations new signal flags for use on opening day. The special ran into a line of earth-moving wagons under horse power, engaged on final work near Hooley Lane, smashing the trucks and derailing the locomotive. There were no injuries, but the line was blocked with mangled wreckage.

Opening at last

On 21 September 1841, opening day at Brighton, the first 'up' train left at 6.45am, but the first 'down' train was the real centrepiece, leaving London Bridge at 9.45am. It was variously

Railway servants – some Victorian cartoons. *(Leisure Hour)*

described as having 12, 13 or 18 carriages including directors' saloons, and coaches for the engineers and their ladies; stuffy little boxes that were then the latest in transport. It crawled into Brighton at 12.15, after 2½ hours on a journey which future generations boasted (geographically erroneously) to be 'sixty miles in sixty minutes'. (Some reports, however, claimed that the first train out was the 9.45am 'up' express, that its distance was covered in only 1hr 45min, and that the 9.45am afterwards remained the day's prestige train.) The invited passengers admired especially the tunnel interiors, lit by gas from small individual gasworks at each tunnel entrance.

Public distrust of trains was dispelled at Brighton in a 'popular demonstration of the most enthusiastic character'. The Union Jack flew from St Nicholas' tower (then visible and not hemmed in by streets), and bells pealed in salute. Most of the stations were festooned with flags and bunting, and local shops were decorated. A public holiday was declared in the town, allowing vast crowds, all in carnival mood, to flock to the terminus. 'Five hundred of the nobility and gentry', with officers of the Scots Greys, were admitted by ticket to the station itself.

Swarming throngs massed in fields alongside the line to cheer the arrival of the first train from London, and thousands more lined the local sections out to Preston. Over five thousand townspeople and tourists gathered outside the new Brighton station, where the band of the Scots Greys, the Musard Band and the Town Band were all on duty, pouring out tuneful patriotic music. *God Save the Queen* was taken up enthusiastically by the huge crowd, after which a half-hour band performance was given, ending with yet another playing of the National Anthem.

Additionally, reduced prices were available for concerts in the Royal Gardens and there was an evening firework display, also a banquet for the railway directors given by the townspeople of Brighton.

Timetables settled down to include one express to 'stop nowhere on the line to take up or set down passengers', and a First Class service stopping only at Croydon, Redhill, Three Bridges and Haywards Heath. Mixed trains (First and Second Class) stopped at all stations.

To the general public trains were still dangerous devices, and non-arrival of any service threw an entire community into panic. Another example of this occurred in October 1841, barely a month after opening day, when it was rumoured that Patcham tunnel had collapsed with fearful loss of life and heaps of wreckage. 'The non-arrival of the first train from London caused the most frightful and exaggerated statements to be circulated,' reported a Brighton newspaper. 'It appears that the mail train, which left Brighton at a quarter before eleven, passed through the tunnel in safety, no appearance of danger then existing.' Between this and the next departure a landslip blocked the tunnel entrance. Messengers were sent to Brighton and

Hassocks Gate stations to warn other trains, and hired flys and post-chaises were sent to Patcham to bring home the stranded passengers, arriving two hours late. Fears of death and disaster were allayed at Brighton on their arrival when 'the most affecting scenes took place between some of [the passengers] who had friends waiting for them, as the general report was that another fatal accident had taken place'.

To close or not to close?

Squabbles with landowners and local boards arose even after completion of the line, like a case of October 1841, when a railway superintendent was called before Croydon magistrates to state the company's case for eliminating a public footpath across the line, which forced pedestrians to cross the rails at their peril. Aware of the possibility of fatalities, the railway company applied to close this little-used path, but the reverse argument was equally valid: that the path was there first, and what right had the L&BR to sweep across it instead of properly bridging it? And who could afford to challenge such a big concern with all its 'wealth and power'? Probably to its own great surprise, the L&BR was unanimously refused permission to close the pedestrian byway.

Rejoicings for the first trains soon changed to dismay at a fatal accident in October, when a London–Brighton train was derailed, killing the firemen of both double-headed locomotives, also two passengers. Appalling autumn weather took its toll, when part of Patcham tunnel collapsed after heavy rain, and Merstham was disorganised by landslips.

Rail and road co-operate

Local road services were quickly dovetailed with the trains, instead of competing, mainly governed from the Blue Coach and Railway Office in Castle Square, Brighton. 'The public are informed that OMNIBUSES leave Kemp Town and Brunswick Terrace every half-an-hour, calling at all the principal Hotels, and leave the Blue Office twenty minutes before the departure of each Train. Passengers desirous of riding in the Omnibus can be called for at their residence, by leaving word at the above Office; the Royal Day Mail Train leaves the Blue Office at twenty-five minutes past 10,' ran the bus company's 1841 advertising. It added: 'Omnibuses leave the Blue Office for all the London trains, returning from the Station to all parts of the Town on their arrival . . . Post horses, Post Chariots and One-Horse Carriages always in attendance. Extra Omnibuses can be had to take Families to or from the Station. Gentlemen's baggage conveyed to and from the Station to all parts of Brighton, or forwarded to any parts of the country.'

By then Worthing and Shoreham were interlinked with

39

Brighton at 9.15, 11.45am; 4.45 and 6.15pm; and with Lewes by coach at 9am and midday; 2, 4, 6.15 and 8.15pm. The main London service was six 'up' and six 'down' journeys daily, running from Brighton at 8.45am (mixed train); 10.45am (First Class only); 12.45pm (goods); 1.45pm (mixed); 3.45pm (First Class); and 5.45pm (mixed), with two mixed trains each way on Sundays. Second Class tickets could be had for the goods train at 7s (35p) for the complete London run. Day returns were also announced to London at £1 First Class or 15s (75p) Second; again comparatively expensive when set against a working man's income of perhaps £1 a week, or less.

Delays and cancellations in those days merited printed public apologies instead of a shrug, such as an announcement of 29 October 1841: 'The Directors regret extremely the inconvenience and delay experienced by the Passengers on this Line yesterday, in consequence of a fall of earth in the cutting at Merstham, occasioned by the excessive rains. They are happy to add that no accident occurred and that in the course of a few days the Trains will again be run throughout. In the meanwhile every possible arrangement has been made to accommodate the Public with Carriages between Merstham and Hooley House, a distance of four miles.'

Already the pattern for the future was set; much the same mixture of good and bad timekeeping, setbacks and successes, which characterised this and any other railway from the Victorian period onwards.

4

Atmospherics and Accidents

Passenger accommodation was, as yet, spartan in the extreme, enough to make travelling other than First Class something of an ordeal. Second Class coaches had roofs but still no sides, open to every passing wind as well as the train's slipsteam and the engine's smuts and sparks. Third Class remained at the cattle truck stage. By contrast, those of 'superior station' could drive their own private carriages to major stations where they were rolled onto special flat trucks to tag along behind the train, with their passengers still inside. The perils of staying aboard instead of stooping to sitting with one's fellow beings were sometimes a high price to pay for snobbery. An account from about 1840 tells how: 'the late Duke of Portland always travelled in that way . . . and (the) story of a gentleman . . . who was wont to go from London to Brighton in the same fashion; once the truck at the end of the train got disconnected in a tunnel, leaving the exclusive passenger seated stationary in his carriage – also in darkness and peril.'

Winter's toll

Two landslips plagued New Cross early in 1842, the second appearing only moments after a train had passed through a cutting near Finch's Bridge. Dislodged earth buried the track 9ft deep for a 140ft stretch. 600 men were sent to shovel up the debris, supplemented within hours to number 1,000; labour was cheap, exploitable and plentiful in the 1840s. Temporary walkways were erected over the rubble for passengers to meet trains which were stopped on either side. Clearance took a month. The slide was caused by extremes of cold, wet, frost and snow, alternating with unseasonal mildness.

Winter services on the London & Brighton Railway were neither comfortable nor frequent; the only 'down' trains ran at 9 and 10.45am; 1.45 and 3.45pm; and four 'up' from Brighton at 8 and 10.45am; 1.45 and 3.45pm, with a mere two on Sundays. An extra service, First Class throughout, left from both ends of the line at 5.00pm.

A dispute flared in April 1842 over charges for carrying mail, which threatened to rob the populace of its day mail train. The argument was that post could be despatched by horse-coach for half the cost. Portsmouth and Brighton mail was suspended until the argument between railway and Post Office was settled. Introduction of a new mail service in October changed the existing

LONDON, BRIGHTON, AND SOUTH-COAST RAILWAY.
FROM JUNE 1st TO JUNE 30th ONLY.

LONDON TO BRIGHTON.—DAILY.   **SUNDAY.**

	DOWN TRAINS.	1,2. Par.	1,2.	1,2,3.	Express 1,2.	1,2.	1,2.	1,2,3.	1,2.	Express 1st.	1,2,3.	1,2.	1,2,3 Par. Excr.	1,2,3	1,2,3
—	LONDON BRIDGE	7 0	9 0	10 0	11 0	12 0	2 0	3 0	4 0	5 0	6 0	7 0	7 0	8 0	10 45
3	New Cross	7 5	..	10 5	..	..	..	3 5	..	..	6 5	..	7 5	..	10 50
5¼	Forest Hill	7 13	..	10 13	..	..	..	3 13	..	..	6 13	..	7 13	..	..
10¼	Croydon	7 25	9 25	10 25	..	12 23	..	3 25	4 22	..	6 25	..	7 25	..	11 10
13½	Godstone Road	7 35	..	10 35	..	..	..	3 35	..	..	6 35	..	7 35	..	..
14¾	Stoat's Nest	7 40	..	10 40	..	..	..	3 40	..	..	6 40	..	7 40	..	..
21	Reigate	7 55	9 45	10 55	11 40	12 48	2 40	3 55	4 45	5 40	6 55	7 10	7 55	..	11 30
25¼	Horley	8 5	..	11 5	..	..	..	4 5	..	..	7 5	..	8 5	..	..
29	Three Bridges	8 15	..	11 15	..	1 8	..	4 17	5 5	..	7 15	..	8 15	..	11 50
33½	Balcombe	8 30	..	11 30	..	..	..	4 35	..	..	7 30	..	8 25	..	..
37¼	Hayward's Heath	8 40	10 14	11 40	..	1 28	3 20	4 45	5 20	..	7 40	..	8 35	..	12 15
41	Burgess Hill	8 50	..	11 50	..	..	..	4 55	..	..	7 50	..	8 45	..	12 25
43¼	Hassock's Gate	9 0	..	12 0	..	1 38	..	5 5	..	..	8 2	..	8 55	..	12 35
50½	BRIGHTON	9 25	10 45	12 20	12 30	2 5	4 0	5 30	6 0	6 30	8 30	8 45	9 20	10 0	1 0

BRIGHTON TO LONDON.—DAILY.   **SUNDAY.**

	UP TRAINS.	1,2,3.	Express 1st.	1,2,3.	1,2.	1,2.	1,2.	1,2,3.	1,2.	1,2. Par.	1,2.	1,2,3. Excur.	1,2,3.	1,2. Par. turn
—	BRIGHTON	7 0	8 45	9 0	10 0	11 30	2 0	2 30	3 30	6 30	8 0	7 45	2 45	6 3
7	Hassock's Gate	7 18	..	9 20	10 18	11 48	..	2 50	3 48	6 50	8 15	8 5	3 5	6 5
9¼	Burgess Hill	7 25	..	9 28	..	..	..	2 58	..	6 58	..	8 10	3 10	6 5
12¼	Hayward's Heath	7 35	..	9 38	..	12 4	..	3 8	4 4	7 8	..	8 20	3 20	7
17	Balcombe	7 48	..	9 50	..	..	..	3 20	..	7 20	..	8 30	3 30	7 2
21¼	Three Bridges	7 58	..	10 3	10 52	12 25	2 50	3 33	4 25	7 33	..	8 43	3 43	7 3
25	Horley	8 8	..	10 13	..	..	..	3 43	..	7 43	..	8 53	3 53	7 4
29¼	Reigate	8 20	9 30	10 25	11 10	12 45	3 7	3 55	4 45	7 55	9 0	9 3	4 5	7 5
36	Stoat's Nest	8 33	..	10 39	..	..	..	4 9	..	8 9	..	9 15	4 15	8
37¼	Godstone Road	8 38	..	10 45	..	..	..	4 15	..	8 15	..	9 21	4 18	8 1
40¼	Croydon	8 48	..	10 55	11 35	..	3 30	4 25	..	8 25	..	9 32	4 30	8 2
45	Forest Hill	8 58	..	11 5	..	..	..	4 32	..	8 32	..	..	..	8 3
47¼	New Cross	9 5	..	11 15	..	..	..	4 40	..	8 40	..	9 55	4 50	8 4
50½	LONDON BRIDGE	9 25	10 15	11 30	12 0	1 30	4 0	5 0	5 30	9 0	9 50	10 10	5 5	9

Every MONDAY MORNING an additional Express Train, with First Class Carriages only, will leave Brighton at 8.30 A.M., arriving in London at 9.55.

DAY TICKETS are issued at London, New Cross, and Croydon, on Saturdays and Sundays, by every Train to Brighton and Stations beyond, and *vice versâ*, entitling Passengers to return by any of the Trains on the Sunday, or the Monday following.—No Passenger can return by an Express Train without an Express Ticket.

Trains for Croydon start from London Bridge at 8.15, 9.15, 10.15, 11.15, A.M., 12.15, 1.15, 2.15, 3.15, 3.45, 4.15, 4.45, 5.45, 6.15, 7.15, 8.15, 9.15, and 10.15, p.m., daily; and at 8.15, 9.15, 10.15, a.m., 1.15, 2.15, 3.15, 4.15, 5.15, 6.15, 7.15, 8.15, and 10.15, p.m., on Sundays.

For Epsom, at 8.15, 9.15, 10.15, a.m., and at 12.15, 2.15, 4.45, 5.45, 7.15, and 10.15, p.m., daily; and at 9.15 a.m., and 3.15, 6.15, and 8.15, p.m., on Sundays.

Trains from Croydon start for London Bridge at 8.0, 8.50, 9.15, 9.50, 10.15, 10.50, 11.15, a.m., 12.15, 1.15, 2.15, 3.15, 5.15, 6.15, 7.15, 8.15, 9.15, and 10.15, p.m., daily; and at 8.15, 9.15, 10.15, a.m., 1.15, 2.15, 3.15, 4.15, 5.15, 6.15, 7.15, 8.15, and 10.15, p.m., on Sundays.

From Epsom, at 6.50, 8.15, 9.15, 10.50, a.m., and at 12.50, 2.50, 5.50, 7.50, and 9.50, p.m., daily; and at 8.45 a.m., and 5.45, and 7.45, p.m., on Sundays.

The sparse Brighton summer timetable of 1847.

(Brighton Reference Library)

timetables, as a public notice of 29 September proclaimed: 'In consequence of a requisition from the Postmaster General to run a Train for the conveyance of the Mail Bags on and after the 5th October next, the following Changes in the daily Trains will necessarily be made from that day:– Trains to be discontinued: the Daily Down Train from London at 3 o'clock pm, and the Daily Up Trains at 6 and 7 o'clock pm.'

New trains were introduced as compensation, including a First Class 'down' mail service doing the run in two hours, and two mixed 'up' trains, taking also Third Class passengers 'instead of the Goods Train', their more usual lowly habitat.

1842 also saw a period of accusation and counter-accusation

against the powers behind the trains, when alleged irregularities in the books were bandied in the press. One printed pamphlet, 'Case of the Brighton Railway Company and supposed Misapplication of the Funds by Persons Connected with the Management', purported to show how a first cost estimate (including the Shoreham branch) of £845,800 in 1837 was inflated to £1,120,000, and progressively higher until in 1842 it stood at £2,152,893. The money seemed to be easily raised; the question was whether it was equally easily spent, asked one cynical reporter.

Accidents to railwaymen were frequent, including one involving the 5.25pm from London Bridge near New Cross in 1842. It killed a London & Croydon signalman who was last seen walking down the middle of the track as if it were a quiet garden path, when a First Class Brighton express came upon him. Despite the guard screaming his whistle the man strolled on until he was mown down, the entire train passing over him. Railwaymen, like the public, had still not fully appreciated the power of trains as potential killers.

Further timetable changes came in November, the 8.30pm 'down' being discontinued and the 6.30 'up' retimed to 6pm. From 1 November the Brighton Day Mail was to be First Class only, calling only at principal stations, taking exactly two hours on the journey.

Horse-coaches still connected with the trains at various points, such as George Leney's Lewes and Brighton Railway Coach leaving Lewes in early morning and returning in connection with the 4.30pm from London. Extortionism among cabbies and busmen created public resentment at Brighton, where double fare was sometimes charged to passengers with more than one small bag, despite a First Class luggage allowance of 84lb weight, and pro-rata to other classes.

'Brighton' bursts her boiler

A spectacular accident marred the end of 1842 on the Brighton-Shoreham section when the engine *Brighton* burst her boiler tubes near Hove with a terrifying bang. People from nearby roads immediately rushed to help, finding the driver severely scalded, but the stoker and a company director who had been riding on the tender were miraculously unhurt. Parts of the locomotive were blown long distances, and her connecting rods were found as far off as Hove, by a railway policeman.

As yet the railway bowed to Brighton's fears of being over-run by loud-mouthed trippers, by giving little attention to Third Class ticket sales or to cheap excursions, but early in 1843 Third Class was added to the first and last services of the day. A few tripper trains were run out to Hassocks for hikers on the South Downs, but London was still attainable only at full fare. Fares were, however, reduced in the summer of 1843 when the

London-Brighton run came down to 12s (60p) First Class, 8s (40p) Second or 5s (25p) Third for passengers, and 22s (£1.10) for a four-wheeled carriage. Such pride was taken in timekeeping – at least, on paper – that timetables warned 'the trains will start at the precise times mentioned' and that the booking offices would close a full five minutes before departure.

Special event services gradually became more common, not least to Brighton Races. For the meeting of August 1843 special return fares were offered by mixed trains ranging from 14s (70p) down to only 5s (25p) return in Third Class; the catch in the latter offer was that it applied to only one train, the midday departure.

The London & Brighton and the South Eastern reached agreement in September 1843 to share facilities at Redhill, ending a period of uncertainty and rivalry, and notice was also given of a Brighton intention to buy out the Brighton & Chichester Railway; a shareholders' meeting was accordingly called to make formal agreement or disagreement.

Other plans periodically flared up or fizzled out, some to go through and others to be lost. Among them was a proposal of the Croydon company to build out to Epsom, likely to meet stiff opposition from the South Western, which was itself pressing to get a similar scheme through Parliament.

Several management changes brought their own repercussions, including a changeover from Chairman Parsons to Chairman Captain Kelly and then to Rowland Hill.

Tolls to the Greenwich Railway remained a thorn in the Brighton's side, a high price for approaching London over a mere one-and-a-half miles of GR track. For the six months ended 31 December 1844 the toll on the Brighton was no less than £3,039. The Croydon company also took its cut, again for allowing Brighton trains to approach London over its metals for the final few miles, demanding for the same half-year £12,793. Passengers carried for these six months numbered 96,573 First Class, 106,052 Second, and 117,559 Third, a total of 320,184; healthy figures for a railway that was still very young. Takings rose proportionately, from £62,672 in 1842 up to £83,799 for just the first half of 1844; and from £103,948 (1842) up to £128,665 for the second six months of those years. Considering that local fares were counted only in pennies, and longer distances in mere shillings, this was excellent progress.

Trippers and tourists

The previously unexploited excursion traffic took a turn for the better at Easter in 1844, when the first Brighton special excursion staggered into the seaside terminus bringing the Cockney invasion Brighton both feared and needed if its trade were to expand. No fewer than forty-five small carriages made up this mammoth train, behind four engines; the notion of dividing

An old company crest survives high on a side wall of East Croydon station. The quartering on the shield represents the following: Upper left – London; Upper right – Brighton; Lower left – Hastings; Lower right – Portsmouth. *(M. V. Searle)*

them into four separate trains appears not to have been considered. Nor was this its limit; at Croydon six more coaches and another locomotive were added. The train to end all trains arrived bursting with Londoners raring to see the sea, stopping only to do a knees-up on street corners as they tramped downhill to the clifftop.

Another monster excursion gasped into Brighton in August, said to have carried 2,200 people in an incredible eighty coaches behind eight engines, but this was contradicted by another report that on this occasion the company had despatched the little boxes on wheels in twenties as quickly as they filled up, having learned the lesson of two previous Sundays.

The timetabled early summer service was poor, comprising only ten Brighton trains including two expresses timed for only ninety minutes. Sunday service was worse; only four return journeys including timetabled excursions. Additionally, Brighton acted as a gateway to France, much as Newhaven does today. The London–Dieppe leg was then timed for nine hours, and the total run to Paris at seventeen hours. 'Fast and powerful steamers' were advertised to leave daily except for Sundays, and there was also a steamer to Le Havre. Brighton men are known to have crossed on these routes to work on the railways springing up in France, cashing in on skills which were no longer needed once their own local lines were completed. In particular they patronised the General Steam Navigation Company's *Dart*, sailing from the old Chain Pier.

45

More refined travellers still had cause to curse railways and the teething troubles that dragged on into the first operational years. Among them were a train-load of people marooned within sight of their station for nearly an hour in 1844, only to be ordered to leap down onto the track and walk the rest of the way. Tempers were not improved by the fact that those who had earlier anticipated this command were officiously herded back to sit and fume in their seats. Such incidents did nothing to foster goodwill between railway and passengers.

Fire! Fire!

Royalty took to the rails as readily as commoners, among them the French Emperor who took his first train ride while in England because his own government forbade him to risk his royal limbs. At the end of his visit, rather than face the widest part of the Channel in particularly sea-sickly mood, His Majesty elected to return by Dover and the Short Sea Route; his special train was accordingly turned back off the Portsmouth line towards London and Nine Elms, where his party was transferred by road coaches to the London and Croydon Railway's station at New Cross for onward transit across Kent. Nearing New Cross, the travellers noticed a fearsome glow in the sky, growing more lurid with every turn of the wheels. Unfortunately they had picked the very night when the great carriage and engine sheds there chose to burn down; a vast inferno attracting half South London onto the streets to stare. The mightly octagonal roundhouse collapsed in a firework display of sparks, opening up the flames within to the sky. The arrival of foreign royalty, grumbling and grunting at the indignity of stepping over hoses, was the last straw for New Cross. With almost indignant haste a train was assembled, heel clickings and handshakes were exchanged, and the station was thankfully rid of the Emperor, leaving the directors free to revisit the infernal scene and count their losses: more carriages and locomotives than any company could afford to lose. This major depot of the Brighton and Dover companies had cost over £60,000 only a few years previously.

The 1840s saw another disastrous fire, at the Croydon terminus of the London & Croydon Railway. It was first spotted by a prowling constable in the small hours, as smoke billowed from a lamp-room. As the local paper took up the tale: 'No sooner had he [raised the alarm] than flames shot up with a lurid glare from a wooden shed which was crowded with First and Second Class coaches, between a dozen and fourteen of which were wholly destroyed, and a number of others being damaged by fire and water.' Brigades raced from London as well as local towns, led by the man destined to become famous as the tragic hero of the Tooley Street fire, Braidwood; but nothing could save the building. The best that could be achieved was to spare the station ticket offices, just as the flames were 'giving them a preparatory licking'. Next morning the damage became sickeningly clear: 'The locomotive depot and the carriage sheds had been entirely destroyed together with their contents; the atmospheric carriage shedding was consumed; the electric telegraph had been rendered temporarily inoperative; a number of wooden sleepers were destroyed; and the metal train-lines were twisted into fantastic shapes and divers forms.' Among other effects, the losses to the Atmospheric Railway helped to hasten the abandonment of that unique experimental form of transport.

Accidents and incidents

Trains meeting accidentally on the same track were fairly common in the days of primitive signalling, as almost happened on the Shoreham section in 1844. A steam ferry having entered Shoreham Harbour, a special train was despatched at the same moment as an ordinary service out of Brighton. Suddenly both drivers realised they were heading into a collision head on, to the 'great terror of the passengers'. Brakes shrieked and steam was shut off, the trains escaping only by grace of the red lights both carried, the only indication to drivers of their situation.

As well as post signals, hand signalling was still much used. By day an arm extended horizontally indicated 'All Right', a green flag 'Caution', and a red flag 'Danger' (alternatively danger warnings were given by 'waving with violence a hat or any other object'). Night hand signals were the display of a white light for 'All Right', a green light for 'Caution' and, again, red for 'Danger' – or in emergency 'waving any light with violence'.

Many of the ancient Kent and Surrey fairs still existed, attracting increasingly oafish mobs by train, among them Croydon Fair. A late train packed with Croydon Fair revellers came to grief in 1844 when the last 'up' train to London Bridge was overtaken at Anerley by one for Bricklayers' Arms, though both were only crawling. The collision sparked off the usual exaggerated rumours of carnage. The simple cause was lack of oil for the London train's tail lamp, which went out and made it a hazard to other drivers.

A glass of railway water

Passengers accused their railway of every offence against its customers, not only of unpunctuality and excessive breakage of pistons, but persistent mislayings of luggage despite the dual passenger and baggage tickets which were made to be matched up at journey's end. Instead, the luggage might be still in London, brought down by the next train – or not until next day. On the other hand, travellers had little services and amenities we lack today; 'a glass of water is always to be had at every station' was the Brighton's advertised boast.

In November 1844 notice was given of an application to Parliament for increasing the powers of an earlier Act for a line to Lewes and Hastings, including compulsory land purchase. A few months later the shareholders met to consider 'leasing with the option of purchase the Brighton Lewes and Hastings Railway'. By March 1845 work was also progressing towards Chichester, onwards from Shoreham and Worthing. The section towards Brighton had already been 'opened nearly a fortnight', and track was being doubled.

The Atmospheric

The most novel new toy was Samuda's experimental line known colloquially as 'The Atmospheric', a major development of this principle running from Croydon area towards Sydenham and later on to New Cross. Experimental trips were under way by August 1845, testing a train's ability to breast a steep incline by starting it from a stationary position up the slope by atmospheric traction. Speeds of 80mph were claimed in some runs. Experiments continued over five miles, both slow and at speed, and on one returning trip a train reached Croydon in only seven minutes, averaging 48mph and sometimes topping 65mph. With heavy trains, the average was about 30-35mph, but again touching 60mph between Croydon and Dartmouth Arms. Supporters of the system were not deterred when a piston fault shot one train forward at such speed as to crash into its own air tubes, scattering fragments far and wide. The casualty was simply hauled away by horses, and plans went ahead unchanged for passenger and freight opening within weeks.

More opening days

Another opening day dawned in November 1845, on the completed Brighton and Chichester line, but it was marred by an unfortunate accident. The first five celebration trains passed successfully, but as the sixth steamed out, two horses hauling a contractor's train of earth wagons approached the line. Not properly controlled, the leading horse plodded onto the line and walked the permanent way until an engine, running tender first, acted as executioner, and 'falling over the horse when between the front and hind wheels, killed it on the spot'. The horse driver was marched off into custody, and the celebration day came to a premature halt with passengers stranded for two hours until a rescue train arrived; hardly the best publicity for a press-conscious event.

In June 1846 the line to Lewes opened with the customary beanfeasts and bunfights. 'Throughout the ancient City of Seven Churches the utmost hilarity was manifested during the entire day,' enthused a contemporary journal, the event being taken as a public holiday. Services to Lewes and Hastings at first used a

Cheap excursion advertisement for Easter 1857.

(Brighton Reference Library)

temporary Bulverhythe station near St Leonards. From Brighton trains ran at 9.30am; 12.30, 2 and 6.30pm at fares of 6s (30p) First Class; 4s 6d (22½p) Second; and 3s (15p) Third, with reduced day returns. Universal Railway Time was not yet in force, as is seen in the company's advertisement: 'London Time will be observed at all the stations.' At this period fares might as well be reduced as raised: 'The Company having the requisite increase in their stock of Carriages, propose to carry out a FURTHER REDUCTION OF FARES' ran an announcement of September 1845. Such reductions had a beneficial effect on Brighton, with trains bringing in four hundred people at a time. On the main line the first London train now left at 7am (mixed slow), with an 8.45am First Class express taking exactly ninety minutes. Next came another three-class service, followed by three mixed trains (First and Second), and others up to 7pm. On Sundays only five services ran.

Tripper Traffic

Excursion traffic was now better established. At Brighton, weekend chaos reigned, with the masses known as 'roaring crowds' piling out in hundreds. At Croydon, crowds pushed and fought into the trains, determined to squeeze six-penn'orth of rowdy fun from every penny spent on fares. On one fine June day the 8 o'clock train ran with forty-four coaches behind three of the line's most powerful engines, the train being estimated to be half-a-mile long. The passenger count was 4,000; the scope for disaster of such trains is even now too alarming to contemplate. Day returns could cover a full weekend, valid for return on Mondays.

By contrast, winter timetables became almost skeletal, with withdrawals and discontinuations.

The logical answer

Still trains used three companies' metals to reach London: The Brighton, the Croydon and the Greenwich; but these independent existences were fast becoming a liability to all the parties. In 1846 amalgamation was put into practice, ending the Croydon's stranglehold over the Brighton and creating a single unit whose name became one of the great classics of railway history: The London Brighton & South Coast Railway, or LBSCR. The necessary Act was passed on 27 July 1846. Notice was given soon after of an intention to push new incoming LBSCR tracks alongside the Greenwich metals through Borough and Rotherhithe.

The first true classic among Brighton locomotives appeared in 1847, the immortal and beautiful *Jenny Lind*, colourfully decorated and with towering 6ft driving wheels. An elegant 2-2-2, she was specially distinguished by her fluted dome in the manner of classic sculpture.

The 8.45am express came to grief early in 1847 near

The historic *Stepney* in early
Bluebell Railway days. *Stepney*
was built as Class A1 0-6-0T
No. 55 at Brighton in 1875 and
cost about £1,875 to build
including the £17 to give the
locomotive its fine Stroudley
livery. The class totalled 50
engines, known almost
universally as 'Terriers',
although the men called them
'Rooters' in their early days.
Stepney originally ran on the
South London and East
London lines, but in the
nineties a lot of the class
including No. 55 were shedded
at New Cross and used for all
manner of duties in the area.
By 1902, *Stepney* had 600
added to its number as a new
locomotive had been allocated
No. 55. Eleven 'Terriers' were
offered for sale at the turn of
the century, but there were no
takers, so they were sold for
scrap at £125 each. 15 more
were withdrawn from service in
1905/6, but No. 655 was saved
to operate the motor trains.
Equipped with a single coach,
655 shuttled backwards and
forwards between Brighton and
Worthing, stopping at every
station and halt. It was a most
reliable and economical
performer. Over 20 engines
were modified for this work.
Problems then arose over
manning with two men only.
The one coach push and pull
was stopped, but motor-train
working with two or more
spread over the system using
three men. Because of the
onerous motor-train duties, 655
received a new boiler in
October 1912 which cost £865.
Stepney had now run three-
quarters of a million miles. She
went to West Croydon in 1912
to work the Tooting to
Wimbledon line and she
remained there through World
War One. At the Grouping in
1923, the Southern Railway
inherited 24 A1 and A1X's. In
1915 *Stepney* was based at
Fratton for the Hayling Island
Service. In the 1930s 2000 was

added to the number to
indicate Central section stock.
In 1938, 2655 went to the Kent
& East Sussex railway to help
run hop-pickers' trains. She
went to Eastleigh in 1939 and
emerged painted dark green
and returned to Fratton. At
nationalisation, one A1 and 14
A1X came into BR's hands.
Stepney became 32655 at

Brighton works in December
1949 and was painted black. In
1954 *Stepney* was back on the
K&ESR and ran the last
passenger train before
withdrawal of services. The
locomotive was delivered to the
Bluebell Railway on 17th May
1960 in full working order
having run 1,396, 027 miles.
(*M. V. Searle*)

50

London joint terminus of the
Brighton, Croydon and Dover
companies, at an unspecified
date.

(Author's collection)

The Brighton terminus of the
then London & Brighton
Railway, with various forms of
horse drawn connecting
transport in attendance.

(Author's collection)

Merstham, when a broken leading axle wrenched off a wheel, over which the rest of the train was dragged while the driver powered on oblivious. For a mile he continued, the damaged coaches jerking and jumping behind, and ploughing up the track. Shouted arguments then arose between two railway directors, who had been travelling in the last carriage, and passengers who felt they had barely escaped alive; the latter believed that the carriages were ancient and unfit for a main line, the former asserted that they were only five years old.

Improvements in services

In 1847, a shareholders' meeting considered amalgamation of the SER and Brighton interests at their common junction, instead of continued rivalry in pushing schemes through against each other.

Trains as far as Croydon were now specially frequent, running hourly throughout the day, half-hourly in the rush hour, and hourly again up to 10.15 at night. The actual composition of trains still varied widely, with some services not open to certain tickets; these included the truly mixed train (First, Second and Third), the all-First Class, and those of combined First and Second. Race specials ran the First Class gentry down to Glorious Goodwood on summer mornings, returning by 10.10 at night. These were strictly at normal fares without day concessions; if a gentleman could afford to race, he could afford to travel full price, reasoned the profit-conscious railway.

Another collision marred October 1847, between Haywards Heath and Hassocks Gate, when the first 'down' Parliamentary train met an express from Hastings at the points. Both drivers shut off steam and the Parliamentary crew, deserting their passengers, flung themselves off seconds before their train cut the express in two with a 'most frightful and terrific' crash. The local signalman was initially exonerated from criminal neglect, but a more serious enquiry was quickly arranged.

In November, winter services were again drastically reduced, including loss of the 9am London Bridge to Brighton service. Third Class was discontinued on the 6pm from London, forcing businessmen to pay higher fares or wait for another train; and fares were a big consideration at a period when the First Class London Express cost a guinea (£1.05), normal First Class 16s 6d (82½p) and Second Class 13s (65p). Excursionists, too, were penalised, day returns being no longer valid for travel back the next day, but only on the day of issue.

Growing assets

In the six years since opening it was calculated that 2,485,788 people had been carried by the Brighton company, and by early 1848 its income was over £500,000 a year. A new agreement freed it of tolls to the nearby South Eastern Railway, and eighty-five miles of new track were open. In 1848 Samuel Laing was elected Chairman, continuing until 1855 and serving again from 1867 to about 1891, a thirty year span, with Thomas Wood as the first Company Secretary; there was no General Manager, this duty being shared by Northern and Southern Traffic Superintendents.

New Cross regained its importance at this time, with new carriage sheds, though its passenger status somewhat declined.

Cockneys to the coast

Trippers were now realised to be supremely profitable, on the principle of small profits but in very large numbers. 'Cheap Brighton Excursions' shouted the hoardings, advertising Sunday fares from London Bridge, New Cross and Croydon of a mere 5s (25p) Third Class. This was an adult male fare; women counted as child fares, at half price.

Even racing was suddenly for Everyman as well as the snob. 'Excursion for the Millions at Unparalleled Low Fares' crowed the advertisements for Brighton Races, fares being priced at only 5s (25p) Second Class, and a mere 3s 6d (17½p) Third. Double exclamation marks followed each price, as if the company could scarcely credit its own advertisements.

The new year of 1850 was celebrated by the speeding up of services, bringing the London-Brighton express run down to only 1¼ hours. Yet still the main stop outside London, Croydon, had not quite thrown off the last of its old country-town character. Great hilarity was occasioned locally by a report of a cow mown down thereabouts when wandering on the line, and 'cut into calves'. The word, of course, should have been 'halves'.

Another excursion peak was passed in 1851, with trains going up to the Great Exhibition, and down to the sea. In mid-August three trains alone carried 3,524 passengers to Brighton, or over 1,000 each. Weekly receipts for this mid-August period reached £16,630, against £13,166 for the corresponding week in the previous year. By then the LBSCR network totalled 173¼ miles.

Number Ten explodes

This was a singularly hapless line when it came to accidents of the more unusual variety, brought to a climax in March 1853 with a famous boiler explosion. Citizens near Brighton station were awakened by rattles of artillery fire: except that there was no artillery barracks there. The stationmaster, in the act of shaving, felt his company house shake as the windows shattered. Rushing to the platforms, he discovered that Engine No. 10, rostered for an early Littlehampton train, had exploded into a heap of smoking scrap-iron. The engine shed was blown open, paving stones uprooted, and one wall of an adjacent bus station was tottering. The remains of driver John Young, stoker John Elliot and Richard Baker, an engine fitter, were blown far and wide. Particularly gruesome was the head of the fitter, discovered in the road outside, and the leg of the driver, which was found nearly two hundred yards away, catapulted through a glass window onto a boarding house breakfast table. The landlady's reaction was 'consternation'!

No. 10, a tank engine off the Eastbourne line, was built by Rennie's company in 1840 and had run 95,000 miles with far thinner boiler plates than were standard by the Fifties. Old and wearing out, she had been so patched that railwaymen alleged there was little left of the original engine. Ominously, she had already misbehaved recently, breaking a connecting-rod and losing her cylinder cover.

A spectacular smash between a Dover-Crystal Palace special and a wandering light engine taken off a ballast train at Croydon rounded off the first half of the 1850s. Four Second Class and one First Class carriage were smashed to matchwood, the heavy tender locomotive toppled onto its side, and one coach was thrown into a lineside gravel pit.

Rail travel to Brighton could now be taken for granted by the great mass of Londoners; their return in one piece was not necessarily so certain, when locomotive, carriage and safety standards left a lot to be desired.

5

Territory of the 'Terriers'

Shared ventures became more common between companies
whose regions adjoined. One such partnership, between the
LBSCR and the LSWR, dated from 22 October 1855 when their
joint track from Wimbledon to Mitcham and on to Croydon
opened, using parts of the historic old Surrey Iron Railway
trackbed. In the same year the LBSCR bought out the East
Grinstead Railway, and opened a single track from there to
Three Bridges in July. Another small link, whose use was not yet
appreciated, was inaugurated on 1 December 1856, from Crystal
Palace to Wandsworth Common, which would open up the West
End once Victoria Station came into being.

Begging and borrowing

This LBSCR tendency to chaperone ailing minor undertakings
undoubtedly decimated resources away from its own main line.
In November 1857 alone, it applied to buy or lease the
Wimbledon and Croydon Railway and the Lewes and Uckfield
Railway; to run rolling stock over the Epsom and Leatherhead
Railway; to subsidise the Mid-Sussex; to add a cross-country
branch from Shoreham over to Henfield; and to join up with the
Mid-Sussex at Itchingfield and Billingshurst. With Railway
Mania at its height, to delay, dilly or dally over some inoffensive
little byway was to let some larger rival company elbow in, using
the minor route to force itself into someone else's monopoly
territory and drain, leech-like, its custom and profits.

Passenger-carrying, even over these secondary routes, steadily
increased as the last fearful diehards deserted roads for rails. On
the LBSCR, their numbers rose from 2,485,788 in 1847, up to
6,811,000 within the next three years. Some of the best profits
still came from day trippers, and the excursion season was well
under way by Easter, with specials leaving at ungodly hours to
reach the sea by breakfast time. A day at Brighton meant a *day* at
Brighton, not, as on the Kent coast, a midday arrival and a
teatime departure. The cheap special train for Easter Monday of
1857, for instance, left New Cross at 6.40am, was at Croydon by
6.50, Reigate by 7.20, and into Brighton by 8.30, before the
resident boarding-house breakfasters were on the streets, or even
out of bed. The return train did not leave until seven in the
evening. It carried a choice between the First Class at 7s 6d (37½p),
the Second Class at 5s 6d (27½p), or Third Class at only 3s 6d

A wonderful panorama of London Bridge Station around 1927. The overall roof covers the 'Brighton' side. On the extreme left are the overhead electric gantries serving the South London lines dating back to 1909. The third rail system replaced the overhead electrification in 1928. Under the great arch of the roof are the main line platforms. The 5pm *City Limited* is departing from Platform 15 behind one of Colonel Billinton's superb Baltic tanks while a B4X hauling an Eastbourne train on Platform 14 will leave five minutes later. The main lines were electrified by third rail in 1933. To the right is the high-level station which was the South Eastern Railway side.

continued on facing page

(17½p). Even for excursionists, the least among passengers, coaches were usually covered in Third Class.

Season ticket holders were another useful source of revenue, the Second Class annual London-Brighton ticket costing £35. During the week excursion fares existed for day tourists, but only in Second Class, forcing the Third Class rabble to wait for the weekend. This helped create Londoners' custom of descending on Brighton in tens of shouting thousands every Sunday to over-run squares and promenades which, thanks to the mid-week fares restriction, were able to struggle to remain fashionable from Monday to the weekend.

For a while the line remained reasonably free of its long-term accident jinx, apart from one newsworthy incident of 1857. Unfortunately for the Brighton, the passenger list included a very high-minded bishop and the Duchess of Inverness, whose best satisfaction was seeing the crew arrested and sent to prison for 'shattering the nerves of a Duchess and upsetting the gravity of a Diocesan'.

Plans for a second London terminus, Grosvenor or Victoria, came to public notice in late 1857. London Bridge was by then

The terminal lines and GPO platforms are empty of trains but the rush hour on the main lines from Charing Cross and Cannon Street to the Kent coast is in full swing. St Pauls mistily rises over the departure of a down train behind a Wainwright Class D 4-4-0 express engine. On the right next to Tooley Street are the suburban lines, electrified with third rail in 1926. A Stirling designed Class O 0-6-0 locomotive hauls stock out of No. 1 platform. *(British Rail)*

under immense strain to cope with over six million passengers a year, and was also cut off geographically from the moneyed yet scarcely tapped clientele of the West End, Kensington and Pimlico. These people were reluctant to cross to London Bridge to start any given journey. The Crystal Palace, reopened in enlarged form at Sydenham in 1854, placed its own burden on London Bridge, attracting such vast crowds to its gargantuan transepts and glass aisles that relief of the many lines approaching it was urgently needed. Pressure on the coastal areas, too, was increasing, and parts of the Hastings line were of necessity relaid in 1858, allowing faster express timings. Season ticket takings had jumped in the past ten years from £10,000 a year to £37,000, or an increase of 270%. This was despite or, indeed, because of many successive fare reductions (as many as nine in 1857), helping to increase custom beyond the capacity of London Bridge.

Spend, spend, spend

The Brighton continued dipping into a coffer it appeared to consider bottomless. It gave £180,000 to the Victoria Station &

Pimlico Railway, bringing its total Victoria investment to date to £337,000, and paid out £15,419 on completing Norwood Junction station (long since outgrown its primitive Jolly Sailor image). From the West End of London & Crystal Palace Railway it retained 42½% of the receipts for working local trains over that short but intensive and profitable stretch.

Ageing locomotives forced more expenditure, for the stable bought in 1847-48 was now composed of eleven and twelve-year-olds, needing heavy repairs and renewals. By 1860s standards they were dowagers, if not approaching senility, wheezing asthmatically instead of with sharply exuded steam. When better passenger stock was acquired, the older coaches were treated like handed down old clothes, the displaced Second Class carriages being converted into Thirds, 'quite good enough for the working class'; the remaining ancient Third Class trucks were given the improvement of roofing. The replacement Second Class stock boasted stuffed seats and backs, which unexpectedly proved a false move: lured by this new comfort, First Class passengers moved down into seats that were almost as comfortable, a good deal cheaper, and no disgrace to be seen in.

Despite a savage 1859 winter and a dismal 1860 spring, discouraging pleasure travel, traffic increased in value by £27,996: money that straightway went in another spate of lesser railway schemes. The Brighton could not resist making use of money rather than saving it, or giving it to worthwhile but unattractive workaday essentials. The Chairman at the July 1860 shareholders' meeting felt compelled publicly to deny mounting accusations of extravagance, and announce that every penny had been spent with the proprietors' agreement.

Locomotive renewals, long overdue, were made in 1860 at £4,229, and carriage and wagon renewals ate away another £3,136, three times the expenditure of the previous year.

Victoria station

Victoria grew apace, its principal expense being the cost of land in such a fashionable part of London. The contractors were required to hand over both approach lines and station by 1 June 1860; but in true British tradition the opening was delayed by late Board of Trade demands which could not readily be met, falling as a result in 'the worst quarter of the year for traffic'. On 1 October, the first train out was for Brighton at 5.45am, followed by an excursion pulling out before cock-crow; not surprisingly for such an hour, patronage of the inaugural train was poor, described merely as 'several persons'. John Citizen enjoyed a railway opening day: but not in October when he liked his bed and the sun did not rise until seven. Altogether ninety-four trains used Victoria on that first day; few by present standards, but a great number for 1860.

Victoria had cost the LBSCR dearly, at over £450,000, so that the dramatic increase in traffic which it brought proved more

The handsome 'Brighton side' facade of Victoria station before the elaborate restoration of 1985/86. (*M. V. Searle*)

than a relief. For once it had spent its money wisely. A complete new populace was suddenly within walking distance of a Brighton train, and when the excursion season came round again they would make the most of it. In business travel, too, Victoria served a new and increasing clientele.

The LNWR made its own pact for partial use of Victoria, linking to both Scottish and suburban traffic. Both companies would find the agreement a bargain, the LNWR acquiring extra custom to London and the LBSCR a new influx of longer-distance passengers.

End of the 1860s

Severe and prolonged frosts in 1860 might have been disastrous but, strangely, when accidents would have been forgivable, the Brighton revealed a perverse streak by staging a disaster-free season, over which it could not resist crowing.

The savage winter of 1860 and its succeeding wretched spring were followed by a dismal so-called summer, but the vital passenger ticket sales did not plummet to rock-bottom, thanks to the desperate measure of further reducing Third Class fares, in the belief that the tripper was hardier than the middle-class traveller. The only ones not to bring benefit to the railway were Second Class passengers, who were tempted to move down a grade and save money, doing nothing for the company's ledgers.

East Croydon: An historic frontage hemmed in by modern underpasses. (*M. V. Searle*)

Third Class sales of 4,874,277 in 1859 rose to 5,568,235 for 1860, not far short of a million more. This was still predominantly a passenger line, as had been envisaged from the start, yet goods trade was proving a more than adequate second income, and when general increases in traffic were announced halfway through 1861, no less than £14,674 came from freight.

Ageing locomotives forced the Brighton to spend heavily on more repairs and replacements, early in the 1860s. Some locomotives dated from 1844, and were fast becoming a liability. Thirteen replacements were built in about 1860 to succeed these dying dowagers.

Brighton's original severely geometrical station began to outgrow its scope, particularly for handling summer trippers. Large scale improvements and better platforms were needed, but even this work was hindered by the line's capacity for calamity; only months after its installation a section of the new roof fell in, following the burning down of the permanent way department. If a building were collapsible or burnable then collapse or burn it would, the cynics exaggerated, with a grain of truth.

Croydon was given yet another station, directly alongside the existing East Croydon, named New Croydon and built over an old ballast pit. It was intended to ease the pressure of local suburban traffic, but in practice had a very short life.

Cheap and cheerful

Cheap tickets carried the world and his brood to the seaside, not only on Bank Holidays but also on ordinary summer days. 'Family Tickets to the Watering Places on the South Coast'

60

catered for four or more people travelling together. As most families were prolific in number, this was a valuable concession to a low-paid father; it was valid for a month or more to Brighton, Portsmouth, the Isle of Wight, Worthing, Eastbourne and Bognor. At every LBSCR station placards lauded cheapest-of-the-cheap day tickets, eventually putting the Sussex resorts only 2s6d (12½p) away from the dingy streets of Battersea, Brixton and Balham.

The Clayton tunnel disaster

The pattern of accidents reached its latest climax on 25 August 1861, when the common run of train meeting train with a crash was exceeded by a smash inside Clayton tunnel, between two excursions following on each other's tail-lights. Scarcely four minutes separated them, too heavy a load on contemporary signalling, and on signalmen whose reactions were dulled by working almost double today's hours.

The Clayton disaster certainly bore out the prognostications of the original anti-tunnel lobby in its horrific intensification by darkness.

The 8.05am Portsmouth-London train, having safely passed into the tunnel, was almost immediately followed by the 8.15 from Brighton, whose appearance jogged the tunnel signalman's memory – too late – that another train had only just passed. There was time only to wave a red flag of danger, but the second train was running too fast to stop. However, the driver did halt inside the tunnel and attempted to reverse back to the southern end, at which moment the 8.30am Parliamentary roared in. A tragic misunderstanding by the signalmen as to exactly how many trains had entered or left the tunnel resulted in the third engine ploughing straight into the reversing second train. The engine leaped like a giant cat onto the roof of the excursion train's last coach, crushing its fragile wooden walls to sawdust. Those who were not terribly injured by the impact were scalded by engine steam, their shrieks magnified by the enclosing soot-stained walls like the cries of the damned in Hades. The interior of a tunnel with two crashed trains adding their escaping steam to the cries of the wounded was the nearest impression of Hell that the average passenger was ever likely to encounter. Worst of all was the despair of ever seeing daylight again, and the prospect of yet another train steaming in, for several special excursions were known to be following. The only warning light that could be devised was by feeding newspapers and wooden fragments into the open firebox door of one of the engines. For half-an-hour no rescue came, until a few poor labourers accidently came onto the passengers gathered in shock at the tunnel mouth, having no idea what to do.

Altogether twenty-three people died in Clayton tunnel. One result was improved telegraphic communications through this

Driver's eye view of the
London-end exit from Clayton
Tunnel. (*Jack Sayers*)

and Balcombe tunnels; another was its effect on public trust in railways, particularly among excursionists, and consequently ticket sales temporarily slumped.

Before the LBSCR could recover this lost revenue, a worldwide trade depression followed, dampening the nation's ardour for travel.

The travelling porter

Continuing passenger train mishaps prompted introduction in September 1861 of a Travelling Porter. He was additional to normal crews, riding a special seat on the tender to watch both sides of the carriages for danger signs, or for signals from the guard, by which he could warn the driver to stop. His duties also included seeing that carriages started off in safe condition and properly coupled, and to note any defects at journey's end in an official report book. This did not, however, prevent yet another tragedy when in 1863 four people died after an entire train jumped the rails near Balham and rolled in a landslide of dismembered parts down the embankment. Being late at Croydon, the driver had put on steam 'at a pressure so excessive as to cause the boiler to burst'. The price of his error was death to himself, severe injury to his fireman, and tragedy to a 150-strong Grenadier Guards troop returning from rifle practice at Eastbourne.

Even the animal kingdom took its share in plaguing the Brighton, when a stray bullock on the line near Patcham caused two goods trains to collide, after one had run the beast down, heaping wreckage and crates so freely across the line that no train could approach Brighton until well into the next day.

Another major railway fire hit Croydon in March 1863,

destroying important workshops 'on the site formerly occupied as an engine house of the Atmospheric Railway'.

Further trade depressions deepened the gloom, notably the effect on European commerce of an American war, which the LBSCR took as an excuse for its poor accounts of early 1862. On the other hand, Victoria working brought rich compensating rewards, as did an upsurge of working class traffic following another reduction in Third Class fares. In March 1863 Haywards Heath station was enlarged and the platform roofing was improved.

New lines and yet more new lines ate further into available resources. They included powers for routes to Mitcham, Sutton, and Tooting; another from Dorking to Leatherhead; yet another amalgamation with other concerns; a new Ouse cut for Newhaven Harbour; even a tramway through a Southampton suburb. The original Brighton main line was almost ignored in this welter of lesser developments. One useful factor was the failure of four major rival schemes for forcing themselves into Brighton territory to steal its potential customers, all of which were defeated in Parliament. They had deeply worried the LBSCR directors, and were also against the public interest; for few country districts could support two railways, both serving much the same purpose, built simply to 'do each others' dags'.

Major events brought in much-needed income to all Britain's railways, especially the 1851 Great Exhibition which first proved their ability to transport hundreds of thousands to one single point and carry them home again. The International Exhibition of 1862 again attracted countryfolk and seasiders to London, placing such a demand on LBSCR rolling stock for special trains that repairs were delayed for six months, bringing the unwanted expense of maintaining substandard stock rather than withdraw and refurbish it. Suburban fetching and carrying improved, with over four million commuters. Four hundred extra season ticket sales were achieved by price reductions. One of the company's pleasantest suburban surprises was the success of a little-publicised West London Extension scheme connecting with Kensington, the LNWR, the North London and the GWR; in its first four months 83,000 passengers from Kensington were served.

Family tickets covering the innumerable aunts, uncles and cousins who travelled in the wake of most family outings continued to be a godsend to scrimping excursionists. As advertised at July 1862, each person could go to Brighton for 12s (60p) return; dearer than true excursion fares, but well under ordinary price. For another 2s (10p) they could go on to Worthing; or to Littlehampton for a fare of only 16s (80p).

In the first half of 1862, 150,000 more Third Class tickets were sold compared with the same period the previous year. This gave encouragement to the forthcoming penny-a-mile policy; for Brighton was about fifty miles from London, and fifty old pence

Old Selhurst Station.
(*Pamlin Prints*)

made 4s 2d (21p), a reduction of 18% on normal costs. Exceptionally fine summer weather played into the Brighton's hands. Much original track had by then been replaced with stronger sleepers placed closer together, heavier rails, and fish-joints.

Yet more schemes arose out of Railway Mania, worrying to the LBSCR who saw them as a threat to their Surrey and Sussex monopoly, to milk off its revenues. They included a Beckenham Lewes & Brighton Railway to cross through Keston, whose exquisite commons and lakes would certainly have been strangulated by suburbia in its wake; and another through Farnborough to Eastbourne, again bringing annihilation to what is today still a glorious Greater London countryside. The LBSCR's own additions drained off more resources, such as a line proposed to run from near the Ouse Viaduct to Uckfield and Hailsham; one to Hellingly and Bexhill; another to Kemp Town; and a line off Redgate Mill, Rotherfield, to Hailsham. Still more were planned for the London end. The total list of pipe-dream junctions, linkings and line layings accounted for thirty-two closely-spaced lines in one national newspaper of 1863.

London Bridge being overburdened with multiplying services, its main approaches were widened, together with 2,000ft of the viaducts leading into it. Buildings in several adjacent streets were bought up for demolition, and a new street was laid out towards Bermondsey.

Receipts climbed to an increase of £77,000; why, then, was the shareholders' dividend not also improved? In its January 1863 report the company forestalled this inevitable question with an inevitable answer: the spate of extensions and offshoots. There had also been expensive improvements at Brighton, where the working departments were much extended. The main boast was not financial but operational; something for the normally accident prone Brighton to blow its own steam-whistle about: it had achieved an entire year without mishaps to passengers. On the Brighton route passengers totalled 408,000 exclusive of troops and volunteers.

1864, however, saw the first of two very similar accidents at Brighton freight depot. A freight locomotive coupling broke to allow the entire heavy goods train to career down the steep incline between upper and lower goods yards, through a building at the far end, and into the street, carrying with it the remains of a wall; it ended wedged into the ruins of a tailor's shop. The companion calamity occurred in 1867 when another accidentally uncoupled freighter hurtled down the same slope and through a storage shed to end poised high above Trafalgar Street. Showers of containers, sacks and masonry crashed down as the brake van stopped at a dangerous height. Once cleared for possible injured occupants, it was allowed to collapse into the road, creating rather more amusement to the onlookers than to its hapless owners.

The City Limited

By the mid-1860s city men equalled seasiders in numbers as regular travellers, favouring particularly the 'up' 8.45am which, from this bowler-and-brolly patronage, took the title of *City Limited* when named trains came into fashion.

A big volunteer services review organised jointly with the War Office created headaches for the organisers in 1865 when, on Easter Monday, numerous specials steamed out loaded with men from innumerable London boroughs, many singing patriotic songs, after falling-in on parade on the forecourts of London Bridge and Victoria stations. The entire complement of 40 to 50 Metropolitan volunteer battalions was to be in Brighton by 9am, an immense strain on a line expected also to run the usual civilian pleasure specials. Perhaps the biggest single money-spinner of 1865 was a majestic Naval display at Portsmouth of the combined British and French fleets, a whole week of 'Grand Spectacles'. For this event ordinary returns were offered all over the LBSCR system with the concession of return travel extended up to a week after purchase.

Enough is enough

By 1867 the shareholders were agitating to prevent the opening of any more extensions and the consequent spending of extra money, as yet more schemes were dreamed up. They included the West Sussex Junction, the Chichester & Midhurst, and the Surrey & Sussex Junction Railways. The damning nickname for

The Bluebell Railway's *Fenchurch* as restored and preserved. No. 72 was one of the first six 'Terriers' built in August 1872. The exact cost of the engine including labour was £1,800.18s.11d. Rebuilt in 1890, it ran for some years on the Woodside line until sold to the Newhaven Harbour Co. for £350 on 27th June 1898 having completed nearly 600,000 miles for the LB&SCR. A new A1X boiler was fitted in April 1913, by which time it had clocked up over three-quarters of a million miles. *Fenchurch* became Southern Railway 636 (not 672) in February 1927 and remained at Newhaven painted black. In mid-1937, 2000 was added to the number. It became 32636 in June 1950 and was lined-out with red and white edging on its black livery. The engine was overhauled at Eastleigh in April 1962 after colliding with a diesel shunter at Newhaven. It was sold to the Bluebell Railway on 13th May 1964 where it is still in full working order. (*Bluebell Railway*)

their kind was 'Directors' Lines'; promoted for boardroom prestige rather than local necessity. Once built, even abandoning them again would be costly, for the directors were by then collecting branches of doubtful value, to possess rather than actually use them.

Fortune turned an unkind face on the LBSCR in the Sixties, the inevitable result of so much speculation to divert funds off the main lines. The crisis came in 1867 with drastic drops in passenger income, and bankruptcy became a background spectre. Salvation could only come from the trade for which the Brighton line was primarily intended: passenger movements. The latest Chairman, Samuel Laing, brought in emergency measures, like offering cheaper fares whilst discreetly reducing the mileage covered on the line; commuters, too, were wooed with cheaper season tickets. By 1875 the worst was over; but this period was a warning the company could not afford to ignore.

On New Year's Day of 1868 one of the shortest lived, and now most forgotten, stations was opened: Central Croydon, immediately behind the Town Hall.

The monotonous headline 'Dreadful Accident on the Brighton Railway' reappeared in the same year, when a box-truck on a Redhill siding began leaking paraffin and other volatile substances. Like the modern cartoon character of a man seeking a gas leak with a lighted match, the guard of another train entered the truck with his lamp, to investigate. He emerged as a seething ball of flame from the blazing truck, the flames immediately spreading to another railwayman who had run to his aid. The first died later of severe burns; his heroic rescuer was also badly burned. The fire is said to have lit up the sky for miles around, and melted the handlamps of the two victims into a fused nugget of contorted metal.

In June 1869 came a crash near New Cross between a freighter and an excursion train taking a hilarious party of publicans home from the Crystal Palace. None of them was killed, but compensation claims of £75,000 were like a blood-letting to a company still forced to count the pounds.

The Brighton Terrier

A great name in LBSCR history appeared in 1870; that of William Stroudley, whose influence on engine design spanned twenty years.

From Stroudley's drawing board came the much loved little AI 'Terrier' 0-6-0 tanks now regarded as the quintessence of the Brighton, diminutive lightweight go-anywhere-with-anything machines. Their characteristic appearance of working furiously with snuffling pants of steam, perkily confident in their own powers, did rather resemble that of a terrier feeling cock-a-hoop. Others might be bigger, but hardly better. Weighing only twenty-four tons, a 'Terrier' could negotiate the lightest bridge and the

67

The historic *Stepney* in her very early Bluebell Railway days.
(M. V. Searle)

remotest branch, where standard engines feared to tread.

Between 1872 and 1880, fifty 'Terriers' were built at Brighton works, primarily for London suburban traffic, but soon they became so universal on the network that the Brighton and the 'Terriers' were synonymous. These little A1s were followed by a 1911 rebuilt version differentiated as AIX.

Examples of these attractive small working dogs in iron are preserved on many private steam railways today, from the Bluebell and the Kent & East Sussex, to Bressingham and the West Somerset; one solitary example, *Waddon*, was taken for preservation to Canada.

The naming of engines came into its own with Stroudley, painted prominently onto the side tanks. Even a simple suburban placename like *Tooting* or *Sutton* gave an air of status; an identity instead of a number.

To Stroudley the LBSCR owed the deep yellow livery, lined-out in various contrasting shades which inspired the nickname of 'Marmalade Engines'. Standardisation, making parts to interchange easier, replaced the many small undeveloped classes which he inherited from his predecessor, J. C. Craven.

The simplicity of outline of Class G 2-2-2 express engine No. 341 *Parkhurst*. Built at Brighton in January 1882 and withdrawn in June 1907 having run nearly a million miles. Photographed at East Croydon in 1902, with crew.

(LCGB/Ken Nunn Collection)

Craven was a despot; Stroudley favoured the humanity that treated men as human beings, in little things as well as big; such as having a driver's name inscribed inside his cab, making engine and driver to be like – in the 'Terrier's' case – man and dog, not man and machine. He rode the footplate and encouraged crews to voice their resentments, or to make suggestions which, instead of being brushed aside as working men's notions, would be brought to bear on railway practice. They talked as railwayman to railwayman, so long as actual familiarity was avoided; for Stroudley was also a disciplinarian. Legend ascribed the yellow livery to this perfectionism, so easily marked that it must be cleaned frequently, and therefore the engine with it.

Stroudley introduced his D1 Class of 0-4-2Ts in 1873, nearly twice a 'Terrier's' weight, yet still very compact; followed by a G Class 2-2-2 of 1874, reverting to the old 6ft 6in driving wheels. Stroudley died aged only fifty-six, a martinet softened by mercy, so deeply mourned that his funeral cortege through Brighton was half-a-mile long.

Collecting stations

Croydon went on collecting yet more stations, with the short-lived addition of Central Croydon. By 1875 it boasted eight: West Croydon, East Croydon, South Croydon, New Croydon, Waddon, Thornton Heath, Selhurst and Addiscombe. By then Central Croydon was already disused. Its site is still identifiable, the old steeply graded dug-out area being for many years past a sunken public garden set behind Katherine Street. Its enclosure walls still have the look of railway masonry.

One of the last series of Class D 0-4-2T built for passenger work at Brighton in May 1885. No. 226 *Westham* is seen at East Croydon in 1902. It was renumbered 2226 in 1923 by the Southern Railway and scrapped in 1940. The whole class was named after villages and towns in the general area served by the LB&SCR. Marsh reboilered and repainted them in his umber livery, minus their names, from 1905 onwards.

(LCGB/Ken Nunn Collection)

Fares fell still more. Rock-bottom fares multiplied by hundreds of thousands made good business sense. For Easter Monday of 1876 a whole series of specials left Victoria and London Bridge between 7.30 and 9am, with little choice of travelling style: either one must join First Class and pay 8s (40p) for exclusivity, or go with the common herd in Third, for a mere 4s (20p) return. Second Class was omitted in this case. As extra bait, the Brighton Aquarium joined into railway advertising, offering admission at only 6d (2½p) for that one special day.

Cheap specials also ran for Good Friday, Easter Sunday, and the following Tuesday, which is not treated as a public holiday today.

Brighton Races were big business, worth putting on the new covered carriages, using them as bait to those who automatically saw even Second Class as cattle trucks. Forgetting its previous 'Racing for the Millions' attempt to universalise the rich man's sport, the Brighton Railway sent out trains of First and Second Class coaches only. Connections were, however, integrated to such plebian places as Whitechapel, Shadwell, Wapping and Deptford, whose inhabitants included so many bookies and betting men that their custom was valuable to the trains.

The Brighton line thus consolidated its dual position as a passenger carrier. In First Class it took the rich to the races and to the great houses of the fashionable Squares. The working class masses travelled in Third, their prime aim being to reach the sea for a ha'penny less than they paid last time they patronised the trains.

6

In Gladstone's Day

Long before trains were dreamed of as practicalities, Brighton was a royal retreat. Queen Victoria continued the elite patronage, rolling down by carriage to breathe the ozone of the town, dubbed for its healthy properties as 'Doctor Brighton'. The railway age saw continuance of her patronage, and the transfer of royalty in general from road to rail. Royal trains became exercises in elaborate decoration, and their arrival and departure points were likewise garlanded, such as the pavilion-like transformation of Victoria station for the arrival of the Shah of what was then Persia. The Shah, sadly, disliked or even feared trains for their speed, spoiling the dignity of his arrival by demanding of the Brighton railway directors immediate execution of the driver, for going so fast that the imperial bones were rattled and shaken instead of cossetted.

Revenue from the general public was reportedly the best ever in 1877, when income for the second six months of the year totalled £1,023,789; over £50,000 up on the comparable period of 1874.

Ups and downs

Today's economic depressions had Victorian counterparts, periodically disturbing the Land-of-Hope-and-Glory optimism of the age. One such period occurred in about 1877-78, very severe and long drawn out, which one would expect to be reflected in railway ticket takings; yet, strangely, the reverse was true on the Brighton, and traffic slightly increased, allowing a useful dividend to be paid, and for a healthy balance to be carried forward.

Bonfire night

Norwood Junction at midnight was the setting for a collision between two goods trains early in 1879, when the second train's driver, ignoring a red signal, ran full throttle into the rear of a freighter which had stopped to obey the same warning. Large gangs of men were called in to clear the rubble, working by the light of flaming bonfires lit beside the track, kept going by splintered fragments of wooden wagons and the remains of a guard's van.

Two minor opening days loomed in the summer of 1880, bearing on the Brighton tourist trade by opening the remaining part of the Tunbridge Wells to Eastbourne line, and also a junction at Polegate.

Samuel Laing, the chairman, could report more favourably in July 1880 than a year previously, when traffic had declined and takings fallen. This reversal was partly due to reductions in coal and iron costs, which directly affected every railway of the steam era. Much track was re-laid with steel rails and, for once, no Parliamentary wrangles over rival companies' intrusions disturbed the LBSCR's year.

The usual technique for improving lapsed passenger revenue was the opposite of today's spiral of increasing fares. Instead, reductions on First and Second Class fares were proposed, as usage of these classes temporarily stagnated compared with steady increases in Third Class income from the working masses.

'Doctor Brighton' dealt its patrons a rude jolt in 1881, which directly affected railway takings, by causing a drop in passengers, particularly day trippers. Suddenly it was found to be no longer a health paragon. Instead, epidemics swept the town, particularly of the dreaded smallpox, which took a hold in Hove and the western fringes. 'Defective sanitary conditions' were blamed. The tourist-conscious council was so anxious to refute this charge that libel proceedings were threatened against a leading medical journal which had described the outbreaks, and a Dr Richardson was engaged to make a counter-report, which naturally was biased in Brighton's favour. The seriousness of the situation was toned down: 'The mortality from four diseases in the epidemic period defined was due to accidental and social as distinguished from any general causes affecting the town altogether, and that the town had been singularly favoured in respect to the prevalence of the other diseases of the contagious and epidemic type.' But independent authorities still thought otherwise; according to one popular weekly: 'There is wanted a far more stringent system of medical and hygienic inspection, with more authority committed to the officers of health.' These claims and counter-claims merely increased the bad publicity, and railway ticket offices suffered a marked decrease in demand for Brighton bookings.

Murder most foul

A sensational railway murder on the Brighton line enthralled the nation in July 1881; the kind of publicity any company dreaded. The popular press gleefully recounted how one Mr Gold was murdered by a berserk fellow passenger during a long and violent struggle aboard a moving train, first seen and reported from a cottage alongside the line near Horley. The body was then flung out into the darkness of Balcombe tunnel. The killer was apprehended at Preston Park on the strength of his appearance: dishevelled, scratched, bleeding from various wounds, and emerging from a compartment saturated with human blood. The body was soon discovered in the tunnel, the main evidence for

Brighton station on two levels, fitted onto the steep hills 'at the top of the town'. (*M. V. Searle*)

sending Lefroy the murderer to a death sentence some months later.

Trade soon recovered after the epidemic and murder alarms. A new all-Pullman train was introduced from Victoria to Brighton in December 1881, running four return journeys daily and – briefly – two on Sundays.

Brighton station could no longer cope with its summer crowds and was clearly a candidate for refurbishment in the current grandiose manner. Late in 1878 some approach tracks were newly laid out and platforms lengthened, followed by a handsome new roof, but more lines were added in 1881, including quadrupling to Preston Park. At the other end of the route, signalling was improved at London Bridge. Victoria, too, badly needed track redesigning, being prone to minor collisions and near-misses, but little was done as yet to ease this strain.

Winter was winter, to a bitter degree almost unknown today, and summer was not necessarily a golden recompense. Many a railway company periodically blamed disappointing figures on disastrous weather. This happened again on the LBSCR – so dependent on casual day tripper traffic – in 1881 when a dismal season badly affected trade. The weather did not relent until September, too late for more than a minor cashing-in.

Fluctuating fortunes

The commercial recovery of the early 1870s had tempted the company to risk money on improving various lines, including those in the Balham and Clapham Junction areas, only to suffer another slump in 1882 when various factors were blamed for a fall in ticket sales. They included bad weather cutting tourist traffic, the continued health hazard of Brighton and its suspect sanitation, and a new nationwide recession. Tightness of spending money was reflected in massive migrations of passengers into Third Class. Like the fox unable to hold his brush clear of the mud any longer in the chase, financially beleaguered Second Class patrons abandoned the battle for outward respectability reflected in the accommodation they could afford, and bowed to the indignity of Third to save their pockets. The LBCSR gave in, and added more Third Class coaches. Even at the upper end of the market, concessions to the recession were made, and ordinary First Class coaches were added to the above-First exclusivity of the Pullman trains.

Rolling stock must be constantly updated in the fight for custom against other railway companies, when passengers judged a line by its comfort. First Class upholstery approached luxury grade, and even Third was expected to be tolerable. The public demanded higher safety standards on this accident-plagued line. Little wooden crates on wheels were an improvement back in the 1840s; by the 1880s the novelty of trains had fully worn off, and John Citizen became increasingly choosy.

Continental traffic was on the upgrade as trade once more improved, forcing the Brighton to spend money on a new breakwater for Newhaven Harbour; but the weather was once more unkind. However, the impact of mountainous seas against the unfinished works was resisted by the new masonry, to the great satisfaction of its builders. Only £30,000 then remained to be spent on this mammoth marine project, installed to increase passenger capacity on the Paris services.

The board members were still touchy on the subject of reckless expenditure, of which the company had been accused in its days of spend, spend, spend on schemes great and small. The chairman felt compelled to add that Newhaven was a single and necessary scheme, not the signal for another outbreak of speculative building. Rather, a pause for thought was intended to let the company recoup this latest expense. Even so, the current rate of expenditure was high, at 48% of receipts.

Gladstone's golden days

If *Jenny Lind* was the best remembered of early Brighton locomotives, *Gladstone* embodied the pride and patriotism of the 1880s; another Stroudley creation giving its name to a classic class.

In 1927 *Gladstone* (No. 214) was sent for preservation to York, as a memorial to Stroudley; an appropriate time for looking back at the distinguished career which carried this engine 1,346,918 miles in normal use, from December 1882.

Variously remembered as No. 214 or 618, this famous 0-4-2

Stroudley's most celebrated express engines were the 'Gladstones', built at Brighton from 1882 to 1891 and totalling 36 in all. The driving wheels were 6ft 6in in diameter, and without leading wheels, some said that fast running would prove disastrous, but the 'Gladstones' were very powerful, speedy and steady. No. 200 *Beresford* was built in 1887 and withdrawn by the Southern Railway in 1929. Fortunately No. 214 *Gladstone* was preserved by the Stephenson Locomotive Society and is now in the National collection at York. After the designer's death, No. 184 was named *Stroudley*.
(LCGB/Ken Nunn Collection)

tender locomotive was Stroudley's culminating creation; in the words of one Brighton newspaper, 'the finished product of a master mind'. For her day she was very large and powerful, of a bold fearless outline and, like most major achievements, ahead of her own time. The driving wheels, which towered to a height of 6ft 6in, were said to make her a direct, if sophisticated, descendant of Stephenson's Leicester and Swannington Railway type of 1833. *Gladstone* itself was generally reckoned to be Britains's most powerful express engine at the time of her building.

This class of thirty-five or thirty-six engines, built at Brighton works between December 1882 and April 1891, for many years undertook the brunt of all Brighton main-line working.

Anticipating by almost a full century the techniques of BR's experimental Advanced Passenger Train, these engines tackled tight curves successfully at high speeds in a manner well ahead of the Eighties. One locomotive convincingly demonstrated this point when, on an express run to Brighton, she was switched in error over points at Keymer Junction onto the Eastbourne branch, veering unexpectedly off the main line when still running at top speed, without shock, damage or derailment.

The celebrated statesman Gladstone was at the peak of his political and national career when this new class emerged from Brighton works and was named after him; some bore names of other prominent politicians. As recalled in 1927 the basic list read:

208 *Richmond*
209 *Devonshire*
210 *Cornwall*
211 *Cavendish*
212 *Hartington*
213 *Norfolk*
214 *Gladstone*
215 *Saltsbury*
216 *Granville*
217 *Northcote*
218 *Beaconsfield*
219 *Cleveland*
220 *Hampden*

Periodic changes and swappings of numbers became confusing, notably in the cases of *Cavendish* and *Beaconsfield*. As a local newspaper correspondent clarified the issue: 'There were in fact two "Beaconsfields" – the one No. 211 . . . and the other No. 218, which was identical with the rest of the "Gladstone" type and was built in 1885 when No. 211's name was changed from "Beaconsfield" to "Cavendish".'

The 'Gladstone' locomotives of the heyday years wore a livery of 'Stroudley Green', nicknamed from a possibly apocryphal anecdote of the period. Stroudley had carefully chosen a certain colour in the belief that it was a shade of yellow and, was seemingly too proud to admit to his own paint-shop foreman his affliction of colour blindness. He therefore reiterated that this was indeed his choice and might thereafter be identified specifically as Stroudley Green. Who, in the atmosphere of Victorian discipline and deference, dared tell the great man that his choice was both wrong and hideous?

Legend also perpetuates an incident of 1882 which married railways to politics, as was almost inevitable if a new engine were to be named after so prominent a figure as Mr Gladstone. An 'intolerant Tory' was the alleged hand behind the ruination of her paintwork, which was scratched through with a file to obliterate the name from the engine.

Later, during Earle Marsh's regime, the old colouring of most Brighton locomotives was replaced by a dull and dingy muddy shade of brown, and the engines' names were painted out. 'Did Mr Marsh . . . so convince his Directors that the retention of names was quite a waste of paint, and also that the engines would look much more attractive deprived of their yellow livery? It is hard to believe it, but it is a fact that as soon as Mr Marsh was appointed, the names began to disappear quickly, and the company's initials or monogram was substituted. The smart yellow colouring also disappeared to be substituted by a drab colour that greatly deterred from the engines' attractiveness'. So mourned a correspondent to the *Brighton and Hove Herald* amid the nostalgia of *Gladstone's* withdrawal year. Yet somehow it

managed to retain its old title when others were made anonymous, like an old warrior keeping his buttons bright to the last parade.

One of this class, No. 189 *Edward Blount*, took high honours at the Paris Exhibition of 1889, when Stroudley himself received a gold medal. Before the homeward journey she was allowed to run trials over French rails, on a line between Paris and Laroche; but for Stroudley himself they ended in tragedy instead of triumph. Either on the outward ferry crossing, or more likely during these important footplate runs, the great engineer contracted a heavy chill which quickly turned into the serious illness that prevented him returning to Brighton. He died in Paris, the city that had so recently honoured him, bringing to a premature end the trials that would have culminated his career.

Edward Blount's driver for the trials, William Love, had previously been the principal driver of *Gladstone*, from her building in 1882 through to the departure for the prestigious Paris assignment. Returning with *Blount* to England, Love was promoted to travelling locomotive inspector of the Brighton company.

Number 240 *Onward* was also exhibited at Paris.

Gladstone type No. 186 made her own contribution to history by hauling one of the first through special trains direct from Brighton to Birmingham.

Many of this class enjoyed long useful lives, and eighteen were still running near the end of the 1920s, though by then with new parts. Altogether they gave about half a century of reliable service, for Stroudley had built his machines to last. As the *Brighton Herald* recalled: 'It was once said of Mr Stroudley that he did not construct engines that could be easily repaired when they broke down or wore out, but built them so that they would never break down or wear out. Forty-five years may well be

Souvenir ticket issued in May 1927 for public exhibition of the historic locomotive *Gladstone*. (*Brighton Central Library*)

considered to surpass the "allotted span" of an express locomotive's life, and we have yet to hear of a "Gladstone" breaking down or wearing out.' Though outmoded in date and dwarfed in size by the new Southern Railway giants, the remaining engines packed enough strength to perform further main-line service. In 1926 two of them double-headed the prestigious *Southern Belle* from Brighton to London and held scrupulously to her modern timetable. At that date their main structures were intact except for replacement of some working parts including boiler tubes, fire boxes, and pistons.

Finally, only 'lack of power, not of pace' consigned them to withdrawal, and *Gladstone* itself suffered this fate in December 1926. She was then bought by the Stephenson Locomotive Society for preservation, restored to the colours and condition of her Brighton heyday. She was repainted to every last LBSCR detail; among those performing this labour of love was William Crick, who had painted the engine when she was newly built; now he was able to work at the same task on the same locomotive in the same sheds, some forty-five years later.

Before moving to York, *Gladstone* was exhibited publicly for six days at Platform 9 of Brighton station for the modest ticket price of sixpence (2½p), in aid of the Southern Railwaymen's Orphanage at Woking. Special souvenir tickets were printed, reading: 'SOUTHERN RAILWAY. BRIGHTON CENTRAL STATION. *Exhibition of Locomotive* "GLADSTONE" *May 2nd to 7th 1927 (inclusive).* ADMIT ONE PERSON TO PLATFORM NO 9. *Available for ONE VISIT ONLY on Day of Issue.*' She made a brave show despite the counter attraction of *King Arthur* giants steaming in and out to dwarf her. A week later she was taken to Waterloo, coupled behind *Lord Nelson*, where she attracted a further 2,108 visitors, again in aid of the orphanage. Though *Lord Nelson* was the latest in monsters, and little *Gladstone* was comparatively small, she held her own to an admiring public. Of special interest was the original Stroudley speed indicator in the cab, 'almost grotesque in its old fashioned principle', set for a maximum of 60mph.

This was the first engine to be privately preserved in Britain.

The long slogging day

An engine of *Gladstone's* period usually had one driver, as a working horse or dog had one master, whose name was inscribed in the cab; he cared for it, maintained it, cleaned it, and worked all the hours demanded of it, rarely handing it over to another man at the end of a shift; for shifts there were none. It was not uncommon for crews to stay up to eighteen hours on their footplate, and take only three days' holiday in an entire year. Accidents to railwaymen were frequent and sometimes horrific, often caused by the sheer exhaustion of twelve to fifteen-hour working days. During 1880-81 alone, the Railway Benevolent Institution (formed 'for the

Historic open sided cars on Volk's railway, the first electrified line in Britain.
(*M. V. Searle*)

benefit of railwaymen and their wives and children') recorded 105 deaths on the line and 1,983 men injured; some certainly came from the Brighton line. The causes of death and injury were many: 'Crushed foot; lacerated leg; hand burnt with boiling tar; squeezed between buffers; killed by fall from engine; back contused; run over and killed; loss of eye while at the forge; both legs amputated; accident to thumb, causing death; neck dislocated; muscle of arm ruptured', among others. Small wonder that most companies, including those that formed the Southern, maintained their own orphanages and homes.

Volk's railway

A very short private railway of great charm, whose pioneering significance was only reflected by the main lines many years later, opened at Brighton on 4 August 1883. For the past century it has been so much a part of Brighton that no railway survey could omit it. Volk's Electric Railway, running eastwards along the beach from near Palace Pier, is a picturesque fragment of living transport history with its antique open-sided tramcars; the first electric railway in Britain. Magnus Volk himself was a pioneer in many things electrical in an age when steam was king; from his workshop came telephone and telegraph equipment and an electric car, and his was the first house in Brighton to have electric light installed.

The spate of opening days had now dwindled to a trickle. In 1884 only the Croydon, Oxted and East Grinstead branch was to open, and the Woodside and Croydon was under construction. The few competing lines bothered the Brighton little, whereas three decades ago they might have rushed men and money into forestalling them by building into the same territory, whether a

Branch line in the Haywards Heath hinterland before its abandonment by BR. The famous honeysuckle bushes surrounding the Horsted Keynes nameboard (now part of the Bluebell Railway). (*Jack Sayers*)

line were needed or not. Horsted Keynes was linked up to Copyhold Junction on the main line in September 1883, and in the same year a joint venture with the SER from South Croydon to East Grinstead was opened.

Friday the Thirteenth

Part of the little Woodside and Croydon branch, since known as the Elmers End to Sanderstead line, built in conjunction with the SER, opened in 1885, as far as Selsdon. It was a pretty country branch that never gained the expected traffic when it became suburbanised. The first house-building developments proved commercially disappointing, and new local residents never really took to these trains. Between the two world wars the branch was closed for many years, except for rare freight trains that earned its nickname of Ghost Line. The badly worn track was renewed in 1927, yet still no regular service ran until 1935, when it was given over to electric units. Again the public ignored them, despite the mushrooming of suburbia. Beeching's Axe almost destroyed it in 1960, but somehow the line staggered on until May 1983, when its last trains ran in to a funeral champagne toast. Many a railway enthusiast noted that this was Friday the Thirteenth.

More mishaps

Reverting back to the 1880s, we resume the familiar run of Brighton line mishaps, this time an explosion in the public cloakroom at Victoria. Short of cash though the LBSCR often was, it offered £500 reward for capture of the perpetrators.

Splitting of trains at East Croydon, sending part to Victoria and the rest to London Bridge, was still common, leading to yet another variation on the accident theme. The front carriages of an arrival from Brighton having pulled out for Victoria behind the incoming engine, the rest stood awaiting an engine for London Bridge when their wayward locomotive, running light, backed so violently onto them when the driver miscalculated his distance, that one coach was wrecked and several passengers were injured.

So rapidly was Croydon then developing that Central Croydon was briefly reopened in 1886 to relieve the burden on both East Croydon and the suburban offshoot into New Croydon.

Public agitation for Third Class season tickets to London was spurned by the company in 1886, in the fear that availability might attract existing Second Class commuters to move down a class, saving themselves money at the company's expense.

J. P. Knight, the LBSCR's first General Manager, left in 1886 and was succeeded by Allen Sarle, dubbed 'the right man in the right place'. Sarle later won a knighthood for his services to the community through railways, pursued with 'such energy and distinction'. He had risen in only eighteen years from the level of a station accounts auditor to company secretary, and then on to the very top. Sir Allen Sarle was specially remembered for the abolition of express train surcharges, 'the perfection of the plan for the transport of large masses of soldiers', and for 'the extension of return ticket facilities'.

The right man in the right place was never more needed than when the expansive Eighties and the Naughty Nineties turned towards a new century.

7

A Farthing a Mile

The solid Victorian world seemed an indestructible permanency, its virtues, vices and values set into the cement of nineteenth century history. By the 1890s, only people aged sixty-five and over dimly recalled England having a king instead of a queen.

National pride and dependability were reflected in the railways, long enough established to be an institution; again, only the elderly could any longer remember the stagecoaches.

New thoughts on old agreements

The long standing strained relations between the LBSCR and SER came to a new head in about 1887, when the existing agreement was becoming more and more unfavourable to the Brighton. Again, the Victorian sense of values intruded into railway affairs; right was right, and the Brighton was conscientiously reluctant to evade the issue and be disloyal to its original commitments. They included one of 1877 when the threat of a London to Eastbourne line had forced the LBSCR to give a proportion of Eastbourne traffic to the SER, paying a toll of £148,050. Time was more than ripe for the new working agreement finally made from 1 January 1899.

Stroudley's premature death, in 1889, ended the heyday of home-based locomotive design. It also ended its most memorable livery, the gorgeous yellow scheme lined-out in various colours and styles which complemented the Sussex countryside with its sunshine tones, and enlivened drab suburbia with a passing flash of gold. Stroudley's swansong was a new 0-6-2 tank engine, of which only the prototype took to the rails before his death. He was succeeded by Robert Billinton, who naturally brought new ideas to the subject of locomotion and produced in 1895 the distinguished 4-4-0 B2 class, with larger (6ft 9in) driving wheels than ever, reworked by his successor Earle Marsh as class B2X. The Billinton family's classes B4 and B4X brought the Brighton locomotive department forward to the last operational years of the nineteenth century.

The human factor

With full flowering of the Victorian philanthropic movement, a humanitarian trend began to be felt on the railways. Companies suddenly realised the truth of such opinions as: 'Overwork is no doubt the cause of most railway accidents; from the very birth of

Class B4 4-4-0 express engine No. 43 *Duchess of Fife* as new in May 1902 at Brighton. 25 of the class of 33 engines were built by the Scottish locomotive manufacturer Sharp, Stewart & Co. and the whole class were known as Scotchmen. No. 43 lasted long enough to become nationalised in 1948, having been rebuilt as Class B4X in 1923. (*LCGB/Ken Nunn Collection*)

the service the companies have overworked their servants, and the results have been disastrous to passengers, and still more so to railwaymen.' A locomotive costing thousands of pounds was cared for and not forced beyond its inbuilt powers; the man who drove it had until recently been considered as expendable as the coals his fireman threw into the firebox. For every coal nugget burned, South Wales would produce two more; for every man lost, two others were desperate for employment, even for an eighteen-hour day worked for a pittance. Conscious of this attitude, the mens' morale sagged.

Towards the end of the nineteenth century, 325,000 men worked for the railways, including clerks, steamboat workers and office staff. Actually working on the line were 160,000 men: 'signalmen, pointsmen, switchmen, gatemen, enginemen, firemen and cleaners, yard firemen and shunters, carmen, gangers, platelayers and packers, head and under passenger guards; goods guards and brakesmen; station men including inspectors, foremen, shippers, checkers, callers-off, loaders and porters. A man's job shaped his whole mien, until he could be recognised at a glance. 'At a large gathering of railwaymen which took place last year (1884) I was asked to point out all the signalmen in the room,' recounted one journalist, 'I did this easily, although I was not personally acquainted with one of the men. I knew them by their careworn anxious looks, and their grey heads. "Oh, yes," said the secretary of a large railwaymen's

A 1922 rebuild with Belpaire boiler of one of Sharp Stewart's Scotchmen. No. 55 was originally built in July 1901 and named *Emperor*. It became 32055 in 1948 but all the class were gone by 1950. The locomotive is moving off shed. The fireman is breaking up the coal and bringing it down the tender. The driver has opened the drain cocks to eject moisture from the cylinders to avoid priming. The B4X class were sluggish performers and never as good as they looked.
(LCGB/Ken Nunn Collection)

club of whom I enquired if all signalmen suffered as these had done, "there is not a signalman that I know in the service over forty, who has not grey hair."'

Unrest grew, as employers cut wages after several trade slumps, and tore up hardwon agreements. On 18 May five thousand railwaymen demonstrated in London for 'promoting the nine hours movement': the fight for a nine-hour working day, or a fifty-four-hour week. Those on the Brighton and Midland Railways were better off than most, with an average ten-hour day (compared with twelve hours on the North British, Manchester, and Taff Vale). Yet still many signalmen, with all their responsibility for trains and lives, worked up to twelve hours daily, and engine crews could be on the footplate for fifteen or even eighteen hours at a stretch. Small wonder that exhaustion accounted for many a signal error resulting in an accident. The consequences of overwork among railwaymen were listed in about 1899 as: 'increased mortality and ill health from alleged natural causes, overwork being without doubt productive of premature death and premature old age; loss of regular rest and necessary recreation; non-participation in home life and consequent non-fulfilment of the functions of heads of families; loss wholly or in part of the rest and privileges of Sunday; demoralisation, the outcome of physical fatigue . . . listlessness [which] adds to the risk of accidents happening to both railway servants and passengers; for excessive periods of labour cause men to fall asleep at their posts, and force them to neglect the careful attention and continued watchfulness necessary in order to ensure the safety of their own lives and the lives of the public.'

Expenditure on wages took a noticeable upturn in late nineteenth century LBSCR reports, as the men at last won better working hours, forcing the company to take on more staff to

Class C1 0-6-0 goods engine at New Cross Gate in 1924. Scrapping of old engines occurred here quite frequently. The rather unsuccessful 'Jumbos', as they were known, were built in 1882 and withdrawals commenced in 1907. No. 430, the last one, went in 1924.

(LCGB/Ken Nunn Collection)

spread what was formerly only one man's load. Though the total takings topped £1,320,620 for the second half of 1889, expenditure took away £547,979, spent almost entirely on new motive power and on wages. The increased income itself came mainly from one event, the 1899 Paris Exhibition, accounting for £34,000 in extra Continental traffic through Newhaven.

Passengers for 1890 topped 43½ millions, over four hundred times those originally estimated back in the 1830s; income was ten times the modest original expectation, now at £1,650,000. By 1891 the LBSCR owned 2,198 forty-seater passenger carriages and 410 steam engines. Freight and mineral traffic increased, too, despite this being regarded as primarily a passenger network. Freight carried totalled 2,870,000 tons, twenty times that of 1835.

Racecourse and runway

Race specials continued to bring in worthwhile income, and increased after the opening in 1891 of another racecourse, at the then insignificant little village of Gatwick. The course owners contributed £5,000 towards building a special race-train station, not dreaming that a century later it would be part of an international airport where jets continually take off low over the tracks. Huge increases in more plebian pleasure traffic in 1893 were attributed to unusually fine weather, including sunny Bank Holidays. It was then estimated that the difference between a fine or wet summer day could be from £500 to £1,000 in booking office takings; a wet Bank Holiday could cost the company from £3,000 to £4,000. Services were duplicated and even triplicated, getting the masses to the sea, and Third Class patronage steadily increased. Yet even Third Class was beyond the means of a shop

Ancient completely dwarfed by modern: suddenly, East Croydon station looks very small (1983). (*M. V. Searle*)

manager earning £2 a week and with six mouths to feed. At least one case is known to the author of a couple who, to save the 5s (25p) fare, instead approached Brighton by tandem cycle, although the young wife was pregnant; the resultant miscarriage on Brighton beach cost them far more than the saved five shillings.

The LBSCR's two greatest inland attractions, Epsom races and the Crystal Palace, were the only ones not to show increased railway patronage in 1893.

Heavy expenditure was made in that same year, when £10,000 was invested in new rolling stock and £3,500 on permanent way working.

Croydon's latest station

East Croydon station was rebuilt in 1894 on a grander scale, under a broad front canopy. Initially room was allowed in front for horse-drawn trams as well as cabs and carts. 'Wide and handsome' staircases were to lead to the platforms, whereas today's reality is the very long descending covered ramps which are the station's most interesting architectural feature. Platforms were improved, and the main booking hall was given a glass lantern-roof. The whole was accounted 'adequate to the rapidly increasing traffic at East Croydon': today, this once impressive building is as dwarfed by new skyscraper blocks as a mouse beneath a giraffe. By 1894, Croydon's boast had risen to twelve town and suburban stations, though Central Croydon had again disappeared. South Croydon was as yet only a minor stop, 'the terminus of a local line'. Duplication of tracks between Croydon and Redhill was imminently expected, after which services would be considerably improved. The cost of this work was estimated at over £370,000.

Timetables started earlier and ended later in the day, until Brighthelmstonians could easily see a London show on Saturdays, leave Victoria at five minutes to midnight, and be home by one in the morning.

Victoria, like London Bridge, was bursting its bricks to handle almost impossible human loads. Adjoining properties were bought for enlargement of the terminus and approaches, and the Grosvenor Hotel (still part of Victoria station) was acquired.

Substantial works were under way in 1896. 'Travellers by the Brighton line who pass through the Croydons and so onwards by Purley to Redhill, may now notice various evidences of railway extensions . . . embankments and road bridges in course of construction, and long lines of earth laden waggons, are the chief features here; and, every now and again, steam-navvies are to be seen grabbing up great buckets of dirt and dropping them into waiting trucks; each doing the work of twenty men and giving employment to but two,' reported one newspaper. Loss of jobs by new mechanisation is thus nothing new. The Brighton and the South Eastern, running alongside each other, still possessed only running powers over the rival tracks; the SER going from Croydon to Stoat's Nest over LBCR metals, and the latter doing much the same, unable as a result to stop its trains at Merstham. However, Parliament in 1894 gave permission to build an entirely new section of five miles from Stoat's Nest to Earlswood and to double the tracks from East and South Croydon to Purley, all of which augured well for future timetables.

Part of the doubled track opened publicly on 28 July 1896, the new loop being intended as a quicker and independent route for expresses to Hastings and Brighton, eliminating the delays which had mounted through the 'busy and inconvenient junction' of Redhill (jointly used by both companies). The loop, when completed, would avoid Redhill altogether, and only slow and local trains keep to the old agreement and old route. Work went on towards completion, but was inevitably slow, including 'removal of a great accumulation of chalk and rubbish' tipped at Marrowfat Lane on the SER part; three quarters of a million cubic yards of spoil were gouged out. Special concern was felt where the new line pushed through the grounds of Cane Hill, then described as a lunatic asylum: 'The railway will be covered over here in order to prevent any of the lunatics who might escape from control from throwing themselves before the trains,' explained a journalist who walked the incomplete track to report upon it. At Merstham a difficult problem faced the engineers: networks of abandoned hillside quarry tunnels, which once supplied stone for Henry VII's Chapel at Westminster Abbey. These historic quarry workings were normally only explored by the very daring, who faced not only darkness, damp and rock

Class E1 0-6-0T No. 161 at Three Bridges in the 1920s. Billinton has added an all-round hand rail and repositioned the dome. The smoke-box wing plates have also been removed. The locomotive was built just after Stroudley's death in 1891 and was originally named *Aldrington*. It lasted until 1925. Three Bridges and Horley were used by the Brighton Company to store locomotives prior to scrapping, and from 161's condition, it would seem its fate had been sealed.
(LCGB/Ken Nunn Collection)

E1 class No. 164 at Three Bridges.
(LCGB/Ken Nunn Collection)

Bottom Right:
A dead E6 No. 32418 is pushed by a 2-6-0 class N towards the coaling depot to have its coal removed from its bunker prior to removal to Hove to await scrapping. 16 March 1963.
(D. J. Mason)

falls, but also 'the undisturbed accumulation of gas given off by the limestone rock'. Underpinning of the existing SER at the mouth of a new tunnel was needed where the LBSCR would cross diagonally beneath it. Shifting sands here must be excavated without disturbing traffic. Huge timber baulks were forced under the metals and strutted up as sand was removed; the timbers were later to be replaced by permanent brickwork. Two years' work was named as the price of this useful bypass line.

A long run of related classes of 0-6-2 tank engines came into service at about this period (1897), similar in their essentials, yet showing enough minor technical differences to be considered as separate classes; these included the E3, E4 (seventy examples), E5 and E6. Two further variants, the E4X and E6X, were recognisable from their rather larger boilers, acquired when the Billinton regime was overtaken by that of Marsh.

Pullmans and pleasuring

Public facilities advertised over Allen Sarle's name for 1897 included Pullman Drawing Room Cars on most expresses; season tickets, from weekly to yearly, available by all trains; through tickets from Brighton to stations north of London, running over other companies' metals; a *Pullman Car Limited Express* at extra high fares (single 11s (55p), return 17s (85p)); and special offers for trips to the Isle of Wight. There were also special London to Brighton returns, including admission to the Grand Aquarium. In reverse, fares from the coast to London and back cost 10s (50p) or

The Royal train behind a gleaming 'Scotchman'. The five coach clerestory set of mahogany with gilt lining-out was built in 1897 by the Brighton company. The Royal Coat of Arms was painted in full colour and is now in the National Railway Museum at York. The train was bound for Eastbourne. *(Lens of Sutton)*

5s (25p) return, on Fridays. The Saturday night 'Fast Extra Late Train to Brighton from Victoria' again arrived home at about one in the morning, at special fares of 12s 9d (64½p), 7s 6d (37½) or 6s 4d (32p), according to class.

Summer holidaymakers were encouraged to use trains during their stay, and not just for arrival and departure, with the lure of 'Cheap Pleasure Trip Tickets' from Brighton to other South Coast resorts and inland places of interest.

Losses temporarily mounted in 1898 due to a widespread and prolonged miners' strike in South Wales, the chief producer of locomotive coal. Without coal the Brighton could not move, and was therefore forced to buy at whatever price was demanded during the consequent shortage, though much of the only available fuel was unsuited to railway work.

To this loss must be added £55,000 for widening tracks between Croydon and Earlswood and expenditure for a new passenger carriage shed at Brighton.

When profits did improve, their emphasis shifted from Third to First Class income, with an extra ten thousand First Class tickets sold compared with the previous year. Second Class sales also increased, with 125,687 more people carried. This was attributed to a decrease in Second Class fares, making them attractive both to former First Class patrons whose pretentions were bigger than their purses, and to those in Third who were ready to improve their travelling lot. There was now little difference between the

90

two, with Second Class fares being only a penny-farthing (⅓p) a mile. Some opted to pay this mere farthing a mile extra to move upwards from Third, while the poorest among travellers deserted normal Third for a lower status still, that of 'Workmen's'.

Cheap Workmen's tickets took all manner of employees to London at extra low fares, provided the journey were completed by an early hour; usually by 8am. They were a godsend to young married men with £400 suburban mortgages on their hands, worth enduring early morning privations. For example, the fare from South Croydon to London Bridge was, for the twenty-two mile return journey, only 5d (2p), or less than a farthing a mile; and a farthing is impossible to compare even with the tiniest coin of today's currency. From Sutton to London the Workmen's fare was just 6d (2½p) for twenty-seven miles return. So popular were these cheaper-than-cheap trains that in July 1898 the LBSCR was asked to put on another thirty or more. The term 'workmen' was only a technicality, for many more than labourers joined the throng, ranging from office clerks and shop assistants to commercial travellers. In a sense the company defeated its own object of attracting large numbers of paying passengers, when these fares became so low as to discourage sales of normal season tickets.

Victoria the Great

Special occasions always brought in useful extra revenue among the sightseer and excursionist classes, as was demonstrated by Queen Victoria's Diamond Jubilee year. Great numbers of suburbians and seasiders flocked up to London to share in the jubilation while, in reverse, Londoners poured coastwards for the spectacular Jubilee naval review at Spithead, approaching Portsmouth along the Brighton route as well as more directly south-westwards.

The late 1899 accounts showed £50,000 being spent on the first five of twenty 'new bogie trains' under construction, and more cash went on track widening between Grosvenor Bridge (Victoria) and Clapham Junction, and again between Balham and Croydon.

Accident-ridden as ever, the company also set aside a £25,000 reserve fund to meet claims for compensation, so regular were these demands. This monotonous theme intruded even into social occasions, such as a smoking-concert organised by LBSCR staff for a London audience of 1,200 colleagues and a bevy of directors from this and other companies (including the Great Eastern, SECR, LSWR and the City & South London) in December 1899. The gala atmosphere was quickly muted by the General Manager's opening speech of sympathy towards victims and relatives of a calamitous accident earlier on the same day; probably referring to that between an 'up' Pullman and an 'up' boat train from Newhaven, in thick fog, which killed six people.

91

This staff concert marked the setting up of an extended company pension scheme allowing all the 12,000 employees to provide for their old age, giving the peace of mind which most working men had lacked until recently. The company's concern that every man who wished might enjoy this special evening's entertainment was reflected in its laying on of special trains to distant stations for taking them home.

31 December 1899 came and went. Victoria was still queen, but the Victorian age itself was already passing, merging into the daring Edwardian period.

Days at the seaside for the masses approached an even greater popularity. This was despite a father's lip-service to his chapel's condemnation of all self-indulgence as sinful, under the contemptuous term 'pleasuring'. Pleasuring to the seaside, with its underlying hint of half-forbidden fruit, summed up the spirit of a century that was dying while a new century approached its moment of birth.

8

The Southern Belle

Ambitions among some Brighton enthusiasts exceeded themselves in the heady atmosphere of a progressive new century, with the most improbable of railway dreams: that of travelling from London to Brighton in just thirty minutes – beyond the scope of anything but a '125' even today. A standard electric twenty-minute interval service was visualised for this pie-in-the-sky progress along a new line from Lupus Street (Westminster) to Queen's Square at Brighton. First Class return fare would be 5s (25p) and Third 3s (15p).

The Brighton General Manager himself pooh-poohed this flight of imagination: 'There is no electrical engineer in the world who would undertake to run a train to the distance of fifty-one miles in that time.'

Much more realistically, the company looked forward to conventional electrification of a line that would readily lend itself to this development, being so geared to passengers. As William Forbes stated in 1901: 'If electric traction is to be perfected within the next four years, and it is necessary to run an electric service from Victoria to Brighton, we shall be prepared to do so.' Meanwhile, he stated: 'We are hurrying on our new tracks . . . Victoria station is to be enlarged . . . our idea is to have a four-track road right away from Victoria to Brighton, and in case anything is perfected in the way of electric traction by the time our works are complete, the Brighton will be ready to adopt it if the new methods can be worked on a commercial basis.'

Cyclists' specials on Sundays reputedly originated from the fact that William Forbes, the General Manager, was himself an enthusiastic bicyclist. Highly succesful, these trains served stations strategically placed for appealing Surrey and Sussex scenery, such as Horley, Three Bridges and Horsham. Fares, including the bicycle ticket, were low: from 3s (15p) First Class, down to 2s (10p) Third.

In general, though, passenger traffic, which had steadily risen through much of the nineteenth century, fell off badly from about 1902. In the first half of that year 27 million passengers were carried, a decrease of nearly 150,000 over the previous year in the same period. The fall was mainly in cheap Third Class sales, so could hardly be blamed on lack of the Paris Exhibition which had falsely raised income in the previous season; in any case, theoretically this should have been compensated by the Coronation of Edward VII, bringing crowds up to London.

Superheated Marsh 'Atlantic' Class H2 No. 423 heading an Eastbourne express near Purley in 1912. No. 423 was built in 1911 and the Southern Railway named it *The Needles*. It lasted until the 1950s. Note the Pullman Car as the train's fifth vehicle. The introduction of electric trains to Brighton and Eastbourne continued the tradition of having one Pullman car in each rake of six coaches.

(LCGB/Ken Nunn Collection)

England had not witnessed a coronation for nearly seventy years – a lifetime – inspiring a frenzy of celebration. Cheap trains were advertised from the South Coast for both Coronation Day and Royal Procession Day, leaving at ungodly hours to reach London early. Passengers were to be out of Brighton by 6am, at Preston Park by 6.16am and at Haywards Heath by 6.36am; it was a very long day out, not returning home until nearly midnight. 8s 6d (42½p) bought a First Class return from Brighton, 5s 8d (28p) Second, or 5s 4d (26½p) Third; these were available only on the specified dates, 'by the Special Late Train, or by any Ordinary Train according to class'.

In conjunction with national leisure organisations, the LBSCR offered lower-than-low sponsored excursions which, once more, applied the market trader's principle of small profits from large sales. 2s 6d (12½p) multiplied by hundreds of tickets was profitable, when offered through such organisations as the National Sunday League in 1902. The snag was that these were afternoon excursions, following up the ordinary full day trips and not leaving London Bridge until 12.45, calling also at New Cross. Nevertheless, passengers still had over five hours away, not returning until 7.55pm. Tickets were sold in advance from the National Sunday League or 'outside the station at the time of excursion'; but as numbers were strictly limited, few usually remained on the day.

Rain, rain

1903–4 saw more Victoria improvements and widening of the great bridge over the Thames which was unexpectedly delayed

Goods took second place to passengers, but still brought in useful revenue. A Brighton to Norwood train near Purley in 1912 behind C2X No. 544. This locomotive had been rebuilt at Brighton in 1911. Note the higher pitched boiler and shorter chimney. The last of this very useful class was not withdrawn until 5th March 1962. (*LCGB/Ken Nunn Collection*)

by problems in digging the foundations. Receipts fell again, deprived of last year's exceptional attractions of the Coronation and Spithead Naval Review, which had attracted tourists in both line directions. Another bad spring and wretched summer dogged most of the 1903 tourist season, so badly that excursion traffic was disastrously under-used. The world loved Brighton in a heatwave; Brighton in pouring rain appealed to nobody.

Further line widening was approved for 1905, as far south as Three Bridges, and French services from Newhaven benefited from a fine new turbine steamer, the *Dieppe*; but goods traffic – never this line's strong point – declined. This was blamed on a slump in the construction industry, meaning fewer consignments of materials, and on a decrease in coal carrying, probably due to increasing use of private and industrial electric power. Some such adverse factor nearly always depressed the Brighton's annual financial position in this difficult Edwardian period.

Hard times

The railway remained in the doldrums, next attributing its problems to competition from the new suburban trams. Trams used very closely spaced stops, running to the centres of suburbs instead of only to their outer edges, and through residential streets. Once established, they made the suburbian dependent on their frequency and reliability. 'Don't worry; there'll be another one along in a minute,' they consoled each other on missing a tram; and usually there *was* another already in sight. Additionally, times in general were lean because of another

King Arthur Class (N15) 4-6-0 No. 798 *Sir Hectimere* hauling the prestige *Southern Belle* past East Croydon in September 1926. The overhead electric lines were first introduced on the South London Line in 1909, but due to the First World War, electric trains did not arrive at Croydon until 1st April 1925. Almost immediately afterwards the Southern authorities decided to adopt the LSWR third rail system of electrification, and the line to Coulsdon was converted on 22nd September 1929. The last steam hauled *Southern Belle* ran on 31st December 1932. Full electric service to Brighton commenced on 1st January 1933. (*LCGB/Ken Nunn Collection*)

slump; so why pay threepence (1¼p) on a train, where there was a tuppeny tram?

Money for pleasuring became tighter, and a bitterly cold Easter and drenching Whitsun in 1905 knocked the bottom out of Bank Holidays; these two bad days alone lost the company about £15,000 in empty trains and unsold tickets. The wet Bank Holiday was a favourite butt of music hall comedians, picturing miserable families huddled into seafront shelters; the reality was that thay simply stayed at home.

The Brighton also wooed the upper classes, and this paid off sufficiently well to allow construction of three extra Pullman parlour and buffet cars, over 63ft long and seating 32 passengers; only 12 seats were allocated to smokers, sufficient before women felt able to smoke publicly.

Short Continental trips included 'Sunday in Paris' cheap tickets and 'Friday to Tuesday Tickets' to Paris from only 26s (£1.30) Third Class.

Brighton in sixty minutes

The *Brighton in Sixty Minutes Pullman Limited Express* gave renewed Sunday services from 6 October 1906, at 11am from Victoria.

A Brighton excursion steams in to East Croydon in 1926 behind Class B4X 4-4-0 express engine No. 67. Originally named *Osborne* after Queen Victoria's holiday home on the Isle of Wight, and built by Sharp Stewart & Co. in September 1901, the locomotive was rebuilt with Belpaire firebox and boiler in 1923. It became briefly No. 32067 in 1948. Note the 'balloon' type second coach which has been inserted to strengthen the excursion stock. (*LCGB/Ken Nunn Collection*)

A new innovation was a 'Weekly Packet' of six Third Class return tickts bought in advance at 25% discount, favouring suburban commuters and limited to thirty-two such stations. Each ticket covered one return trip to London on the date printed, or earlier within the specified week. Season ticket prices were reduced from the South Coast in 1907.

New rolling stock was ordered: five fine vestibule carriages with a parlour saloon, lit by electricity from a dynamo and accumulators on board. Instead of fixed upholstered seating, passengers enjoyed individual wicker chairs, movable as they pleased; they could also control their own electric lights. By spring 1907 these coaches were operational on the 8.45am and 9.55am ex-Brighton. No surcharges were made, only normal fares.

The Southern Belle

A major named train emerged in November 1908, the glamorous *Southern Belle*. This train – 'nothing more elegant, more luxuriously comfortable, has ever been devised by railway experts' – began by carrying guest celebrities on the planned one-hour run. The coaches aroused Press raptures: 'The hand of the decorator has been laid lightly upon this work, and the beauty of

97

The 1.55 pm Victoria –
Brighton. September 1921.
(*LCGB/Ken Nunn Collection*)

it is a beauty that will endure. There are costly woods, exquisite inlayings, elegant electric fittings, and delicate upholstering; but nowhere is there mere display. It is a Pullman train beautified, and the traveller walking through its whole length of seven cars – they are vestibuled throughout – will find a new delight in every car,' wrote one journalist. Among the named carriages were *Cleopatra*, *Belgravia*, *Bessborough* (named after the Chairman and decorated in Adam style), *Princess Helen* (in 'plum pudding' mahogany), the smaller brake-parlour cars *Alberta* and *Verona*, in French Renaissance manner, and the *Grosvenor* buffet, richly inlaid with satinwood. The *Belle* was more palace than train, carrying 219 passengers in luxury.

The inaugural train carried the mayors of Brighton and Hove, Corporation members, and the Press, lavishly entertained en route. On arrival they transferred to the Metropole Hotel for a luncheon chaired by Lord Bessborough. 'No speeches' boasted the menu, and commendably, speaking was indeed limited to four toasts. Proposing 'success to the *Southern Belle*', the Chairman commended the driver on the down journey before outlining the train's main purpose: 'to improve the quality of the traffic to Brighton' – or, rather, the quality of The Quality, who alone could afford it. Brighton was all too synonymous with raucous day trippers: the *Belle* might restore the clientele of the old Royal Pavilion days.

On 1 November 1908 came the first public run. All seats being taken long before eleven o'clock, a duplicated *Pullman Limited* was mustered as a follow-up. Crowds packed Brighton terminus to see the elegant arrivals, including 'a number of very stylishly dressed ladies', drawing gasps from such domestics and shopgirls

An up goods near Purley in July 1919 hauled by Class C3 0-6-0 goods engine No. 302. One of Marsh's first designs, it incorporated many Billinton features such as cab, chimney and smokebox, but with a larger 170lb per sq.in. boiler. There were only ten in the class, being built in 1906; most had gone by the end of the last war, and the last went in 1952. They were inclined to run hot at speed.

(*LCGB/Ken Nunn Collection*)

as could cadge time off. The ladies' dignity was somewhat diminished when the second *Pullman Limited* coasted in so soon after the main *Belle* that the depleted cab rank could not cope with them, forcing them to walk to their destinations.

The *Southern Belle*, steam heated and superbly ventilated, was considered the most luxurious railway train in Britain. Usually she was headed by a large tender locomotive of the *Atlantic* type.

Electrification

Increasing tram competition was among the issues forcing electrification to be further considered, especially in the suburbs, aiming to recapture short distance travellers. The short inner-London loop from Victoria round to London Bridge was an early choice for adaptation, on the overhead cable and not third-rail system. Power would come from the London Electric Supply Company at Deptford, east of London Bridge, and repair shops were planned for a wasteland area near Peckham Rye (where later, in the 1950s, *Brighton Belle* electric units could be seen parked on a raised siding). Delays inevitably dogged the work, caused partly by low bridges which made threading through of the overhead cables difficult, and partly by problems in putting supporting pylons into narrowly confined embankments. Board of Trade safety regulations caused further holdups, the objection being that certain signals were masked to the view of drivers by the tangle of thick overhead cables. Test trains, however, kept running on the Battersea Park to Peckham Rye section, testing both equipment and train units, and training motormen who had been reared on steam. The first major test run, on 31 January

0-6-2T Class E6 built at Brighton in 1905 just after the death of R. J. Billinton. His successor did not bestow names on freight locos, and 417 was always painted black, never wearing the Stroudley Green nor the Marsh umber. Here she is in her last days rusting away prior to withdrawal, but still has the warning flash of overhead wires affixed to her tanks. It could be that the last duty of this loco was a cross-London freight to the London Midland Region with its 25Kv overhead system, hence the need for the warning.

(D. J. Mason)

1909, took Lord Bessborough, the Chairman, and William Forbes, the General Manager, with other notabilities, from Battersea Park to East Brixton and back; a short taste of the reality of electric trains.

High summer

1910 summer services included many extra trains aimed at day trippers, and other services were speeded up and improved in number. *Southern Belle* departures were announced as two return trips daily, running in the sixty minutes which were the advertising department's proudest boast, now leaving Victoria at 11am and 3.10pm, returning from Brighton at 12.20 and 5.45pm.

Douglas Earle Marsh, on taking charge of the locomotive department, found the Brighton stable overbalanced in having massive luxury rolling stock and heavy excursion trains, with few heavyweight locomotives to haul them at speed. His short-term answer was to acquire plans of existing Great Northern 'Atlantics' and have them remade as a new class: 4-4-2 H1 and H2 of 1905 and 1911 respectively, both destined for half-a-century's working. 1906 brought in his L1 4-4-2 tank engine, a most useful all-rounder. He rebuilt some surviving Stroudley 'Terriers' from 1911 onwards as the modified AIX class.

In the back of Brighton shed lurks E4 No. 32468, with both cylinders out. The date is 7 October 1962 and 468 will never steam again. (*D. J. Mason*)

On strike

When Earle Marsh fell too ill to continue, the name of Billinton reappeared, in the son Lawson Billinton, the LBSCR's final locomotive engineer before losing its separate identity. His contributions included the 4-6-2T class J heavy locomotive of 89 tons, and his class L of 1914, another heavyweight of over 98 tons.

A major strike paralysed Britain in 1911, with 200,000 railwaymen idle over the pay issue; 80,000 of them were said to earn only £1 a week, or even less, for gruelling hours on the line.

Also in 1911, estimates were taken for electrifying the whole Brighton line. By then suburban electric working was well advanced, probing out to Norwood Junction.

Last years of peace

Immediately before the First World War services reached a peak, with the *Southern Belle* being supplemented by a dozen other Pullman or part-Pullman trains. Bank Holidays were a greater plebian uproar than ever, the beaches described as 'black with people'. The *Sunny South Specials*, equivalent to the later *Sunny South Expresses*, ferried additional crowds of Northerners to the South Coast, to add Yorkshire and Lancashire accents to the prevailing Cockney. Some could afford short holidays, at

Class E5X Radial tank No. 32586 seen in 1949. No. 586 was built in 1903 and was called *Maplehurst*. In 1909 it was converted into a 2-4-2T as Mr. Marsh disliked leading driving wheels on passenger engines, but within a short time it reverted to 0-6-2 wheel arrangement. In 1911 Marsh tried another experiment and put Class C3 on 586 and re-classified it as E5X in which state it lasted until the early years of nationalisation.
(*P. J. Tyrrell*)

boarding houses charging 25s (£1.25) a week for full board, probably with the use of a billiards table, a smoking room, and – the landlady's proudest boast – 'electric light in all rooms'.

The First World War

Those final summer trippers acted almost as if they knew this was their last normal season, before the outbreak of war changed life within days.

State control of railways was assumed from 4 August 1914, taking the LBSCR from its own directors' hands into a nationwide pool of men, engines and permanent way whose prime consideration would now be troops and munitions instead of excursionists. A War Railway Council already existed, including Military, Admiralty and Board of Trade representatives. Actual operations came under a Railway Executive Committee, composed of the General Managers of the principal peacetime companies. Cheap excursion advertisements vanished, replaced by exhortations to join the forces: 'Your Country Needs You . . . God Save the King.' Many services were suspended, but by October some were restored, including the *Belle*, like a cocking of a contemptuous Pullman-coloured thumb at the Hun. Some excursions were revived in time for a taste of late summer sunshine. But, returning to Victoria, the trippers were forcibly reminded that war existed, by groups of soldiers continually on the move. Later, men with the horror of

A Royal Special to Epsom
Downs in 1911, hauled by
Class 13 4-4-2T No. 78.
Marsh's superheated 'Atlantic'
tanks emerged from Brighton
works; No. 78 was built in
October 1910. The class were
best known for their work
running the *Sunny South
Expresses*. A non-stop section
from East Croydon to Rugby
was run on one tank-full of
water, and one bunker of fuel,
averaging 27lbs of coal per
mile. An extremely economical
result compared with the
unsuperheated 'Precursor'
Class locomotive of the
L&NWR. (*LCGB/Ken Nunn
Collection*)

Flanders in their eyes came through for a few days' leave to be
frantically enjoyed before returning to Europe. They descended
noisily on the Soldiers' Refreshment Room, staffed by buxom
Cockney women and having such added homely 'comforts' as
recent newspapers.

The Queen's cup of tea

Queen Alexandra herself reputedly took occasional turns of duty
in a similar canteen at London Bridge. There she doled out tea and
coffee alongside working class women from the poorest streets,
united with them in serving a stream of servicemen who rarely, if
ever, recognized her; for who would expect to receive his 'cuppa'
from the Queen?

Lady Limerick's Free Refreshment Buffet for servicemen at
London Bridge inspired much fund raising, including special
matinees and variety shows at London theatres.

Down at Brighton, wounded troops used the Royal Pavilion as a
hospital, which dealt with about 35,000 cases, and the LBSCR
handled some 200 ambulance trains. The engine-shop turned
partly to munitions, producing thousands of hand grenades.

Halfway through the war, passenger services were drastically
cut and some stations closed, including Kemp Town. No fewer
than ninety-five Sunday trains disappeared, but weekday rush
hour services were less badly affected; already grossly
overcrowded, they could scarcely be further pruned. The LBSCR

was also forbidden to run its 'Special Horse Trains' to Gatwick races, forcing horseboxes onto the roads.

For the fallen

Men in non-footplate and non-signalling grades left for the Front, and were temporarily replaced by women clerks and cleaners. Some were never to return. At a company Act of Remembrance held in 1917 their numbers were put at over 4,300, of whom 277 died and over 300 were wounded; thirty had by then been decorated for war gallantry. A minute's silence was observed in their honour by fellow railwaymen.

After the Armistice an unusual tribute was made to the LBSCR men, in the naming of its 'War Memorial Engine', the 4-6-4 tank *Remembrance*.

Peace returns

Passenger travel again expanded after the war, until stations were often overburdened. Deptford Council made a request for better facilities at New Cross, where inadequacies were alleged to be a public danger.

Holidaymaking revived, though at higher cost; 'Mrs . . . 's High Class Boarding Establishment' could now command 2½ guineas (£2.62½) a week, and a good hotel 3 guineas (£3.15)

Supplementary fares imposed for subsidising the war effort lingered on into 1919, an iniquitous imposition to travellers counting every penny. The normal Brighton fare was thus quoted as '1st 8s 6d (42½p),3rd 4s 2½d (21p) plus War Supplement'.

Patriotism was replaced by everyday discontent and another major rail strike loomed, so paralysing that Government intervention was expected for requisitioning cars and carts for freight carrying. Troops were to patrol vulnerable yards, volunteers had to be protected against belligerent strikers, and food rationing was reintroduced. Army leave was stopped, and men awaiting 'demob' after the war were forced to delay their return to Civvy Street while the national emergency lasted.

Whatever else had changed, dissatisfied human nature was still the same.

9

The Landmark Years

Electrification was still essentially a suburban issue as the 1920s opened, creating increasing frustration among longer-distance steam-train travellers to whom services appeared only to worsen. The currently fashionable plea of bad locomotive coal seemed a poor excuse for breakdowns, though to the company it was only too true. On one especially fraught day of June 1921, for example, the troubles of the 7.15am Hove-London train extended to a 2½-hour crawl for a fifty mile 'Express' run. They embraced breakdown of its engine at Three Bridges due to poor coal; transfer of the passengers to an incoming Eastbourne train; breakdown of the Eastbourne train at Horley; re-coaling and re-watering at the same stop; and more mechanical troubles at Earlswood. The 7.15 finally reached London Bridge at 9.56am, amusing neither to the passengers nor to the company.

Pullman and Princess

In the autumn of 1921, Second Class Pullmans were added to the boat-trains leaving from Victoria at 10am and 8.20pm. Continental services were then the only ones carrying Second Class, this class of travel having been abolished long since on all other services. Third Class Pullmans existed on principal South Coast runs, an amenity which was expected to be further developed.

Royal events nearly always benefited the company, by attracting spectators to travel up to the London decorations and ceremonial. The marriage in February 1922 of Princess Mary was no exception, and brought people from rather further away than Brighton as an extra source of railway profit. For four days running, the Brighton company, in league with French State Railways, handled special wedding excursions from Paris to London via Newhaven, leaving the French capital twice daily, at 10am and 9.05pm. During this same month additional specials brought Parisiens to London for a major rugby match at Twickenham. By modern standards, return fares were extremely low, ranging from 81s 10d (£4.09) in First Class, down to only 40s 10d (£2.04) in Third.

Landmark year

1923 was a universal railway landmark year for Britain, when the Grouping (amalgamation) brought most of the existing individual railway companies together into only four main

Colonel L. B. Billinton was responsible for the most powerful Brighton locomotives, Class K 2-6-0 heavy goods. Seen here is No. 347 at New Cross Gate in April 1925, fitted with top-feed dome and fully lined-out in SR livery. It was built in 1920 and lasted until withdrawal on 7 January 1963. No. 347 was uniquely fitted with pop safety valves.
(*LCGB/Ken Nunn Collection*)

categories, the Big Four (GWR, LNER, LMSR and SR). From 1 January 1923 the former LBSCR therefore ceased to exist as a separate entity, absorbed together with the LSWR and SECR into the giant Southern Railway, under one supreme head, Sir Herbert Walker.

It was not long before Brighton Corporation, seeing electrification spreading through the London suburbs, but as yet coming nowhere near the sea, sent a formal deputation to agitate the Southern into action, only to be conclusively rebuffed. Not until all suburban electrification was completed would the Southern consider moving outwards; and even then, any improvement would be in frequency of services rather than speed, keeping still to the old standard timing of sixty minutes.

However, by 1925 electric services had moved a little in the right direction, by reaching Coulsdon North. But for long distance haulage, steam was still the standard motive power. The 'River' class engines (including such Sussex placenames as *River Adur* and *River Arun*) having proved unsatisfactory on the Brighton line, some of the magnificent new 'King Arthur' class were brought in, backing up the older 'Remembrance' class and the 'Atlantics'. The SR 'King Arthur' class of 4-6-0 tender engines appeared in 1926, reviving the tradition of named locomotives with characters of King Arthur's court: *Excalibur, King Uther, Merlin, Morgan le Fay, Queen Guinevere, Sir Launcelot,* and many more evocative titles. The romance of Camelot and the romance of steam proved to be no uneasy bedfellows.

The Southern Railway classified No. 325 as J1. It is seen at East Croydon in the first years of the grouping, when standards of engine cleanliness were beginning to fail. The Southern later painted both 325 and 326 in Malachite Green and added 2000 to their numbers, but unfortunately removed their names.
(LCGB/Ken Nunn Collection)

The General Strike

One of Britain's gravest industrial crises developed in 1926: the bitter General Strike born on 3 May out of a protracted coalfield dispute. It gripped nearly every transport system, forcing young secretaries to walk up to five miles to work, and thousands of weekend cyclists to take their machines onto the weekday roads. Trams and trains stood idle until volunteers could be mustered to run skeleton services whose overcrowding made the normal rush-hour look like a quiet Sunday picnic. Not until 12 May was the strike's vicious grip broken, followed by a message to the nation from the King and a gradual reawakening of normality.

After such rigours, Londoners were keener than ever to enjoy themselves, so long as this could be done cheaply, and when a super-heatwave blistered Brighton later in 1926 they responded by pouring down in tens of thousands: by bicycle and tandem, in the growing army of little black cars, but principally in the traditional way, by train. They jammed into the small compartments to endure stifling heat for the reward of a few seaside hours away from the humidity and dirt of London. Hundreds, tempted by the oven heat lingering into dusk, abandoned the prospect of sweating suburbia and slept rough on the Brighton beaches, slumped into deckchairs or sprawled flat on the pebbles. Bathing resumed at early dawn, so hot was the air. The bitterness of the General Strike, and the harshness of working long hours for only £2 a week, were alike forgotten, as Brighton basked without a care.

Excursion traffic remained the jam of profit on the Brighton's bread-and-butter commuter carrying, rising to ever new heights as wages gradually improved and a few days' annual holiday became generalised. Trippers came not only from the south but from the Midlands and north as well, by such services as the *Sunny South Expresses*, the Brighton section of which was often in charge of a geriatric but still serviceable 'Gladstone'. Trains from other parts of the Southern executed complicated reversals to reach the Queen of Watering Places. For instance, we know of a through train from Sheerness in Kent which reversed at least three times (at Sittingbourne, Strood and Tonbridge, and possibly also at Lewes). Its full-length roofboards are remembered as reading 'Sheerness-Tonbridge-Tunbridge Wells-Brighton'.

Brighton station, in popular parlance, was 'bursting at the seams' with tourists, and during the ten-week high season was said to handle anything from two to three million passengers. The drastic action needed to increase its capacity was undertaken early in 1927, when some £90,000 worth of work was put in hand. The main concourse between the outer walls and the ticket barriers was enlarged; better cloakroom and left luggage facilities were installed; improved staff rooms for porters and guards were made; and the enquiry offices and waiting rooms were improved.

March 1963 saw Brighton Shed yard almost empty of locomotives. In the foreground are a 2-6-0 Class N and a Standard 4-6-0 Class 4, equipped with a double chimney, No. 75068.
(D. J. Mason)

Ladies Only

Ladies Only compartments, usually differentiated by green window labels, were a familiar Brighton line feature, much used by women travelling alone, especially after dark, and mindful of various well publicised railway murders and lesser assaults. A man forcing his way into a Ladies Only carriage faced a fine as surely as if he had wrongfully pulled the communication cord or punched a railway servant. No serious breach of this rule was actually taken to court until 1921, when a male season ticket holder was fined 40s (£2) plus costs for travelling by Ladies Only accommodation without clearance from the guard. These compartments were usually placed next door to the guard's van, so that screams for help could be readily heard.

Wind and weather

Severe winter flooding in January 1928 cost the company dearly in damage and in lost fares, as rivers rose and overflowed and tracks were damaged. Torrential rain brought down about 1,500 tons of muddy earth onto the line between Coulsdon and Merstham, closing it for many hours. Only shuttle services could be maintained, from Merstham to Earlswood, where fast trains were specially stopped to pick up passengers stranded by the landslip.

109

The pathos of waiting for the end. No. 32328 *Hackworth* shunted into Eastleigh works for scrapping in the 1950s. Sadly the Southern Railway had no further use for the splendid 'Baltic' tanks after electrification, but they were loathe to throw anything away, so the seven locomotives were rebuilt in 1934 as 4-6-0 tender engines classified N15X, and put to work on the Western Section out of Nine Elms. They proved mediocre performers and most had gone by the mid 1950s, but *Beattie* mouldered away for some time at Basingstoke in the down side bay until the summer of 1957. (*LCGB/Ken Nunn Collection*)

Though the chalk and gravel blocking the way were tackled by large gangs of labourers, working all night as well as all day to clear the rubble and shore up the slipping embankments, delays were inevitable.

Nature always posed engineering problems in the North Downs and Wealden country, where the earth was loose and inclined to slip, and had unexpected boggy patches even at quite high altitudes, which posed their own hazards. The story is still in popular circulation of locomotive breaking activities near Horley when, following a derailment, an engine is said to have plunged off the line and into one such morass, gradually sinking under its own weight into the shifting mud until completely swallowed. It was considered not worth rescuing and is said to be there to this day, entombed. The tale rings true; there is another story about similar marshy countryside on the former Somerset & Dorset Railway where a derailed engine is widely held to be lying under a lineside bog. Bogs like this also tended to smoulder when fired by sparks and cinders from passing steam trains; a further Surrey tradition remembers a lineside peat bog near Redhill which, following the action of locomotive sparks, smouldered under the surface for months on end.

The Belle's birthday

The *Southern Belle's* twenty-first birthday was celebrated in November 1929 with special events and functions, and with decorations at the London and Brighton termini. The actual commemoration train was hauled in by the noble *Sir Ontzlake*, carrying a complement of special passengers who afterwards celebrated with a luncheon at the Royal Albion Hotel.

During the sixties, many special steam trains were run to say farewell to either a line being closed under the Beeching axe, or to a favourite class of engine becoming extinct. Brighton shed serviced specials that came to this part of Sussex. On 7 October 1962, a visitor from Basingstoke, 'Schools' Class 4-4-0 No. 30925 *Cheltenham*, was receiving attention at Brighton. Luckily 30925 has been preserved and is part of the National collection of steam locomotives.
(D. J. Mason)

Another 'School' awaits scrapping at Hove goods yard. No. 30915 was named after the famous Brighton public school. But as on other withdrawn locos the nameplate has been removed along with the Shed Code, and also the coupling rods, so that it will not seize up when eventually moved.
(D. J. Mason)

Early Closing Day

One movement for the public good which affected railway workings was the Early Closing campaign. For many years the arduous hours worked by shop assistants had been a social scandal. Often they were forced to stay open until ten or even eleven o'clock at night. Their only day off was therefore Sunday; still not really meant for 'pleasuring' instead of going to chapel, unless they travelled with an underlying sense of guilt. The Voluntary Early Closing Association was one of many organisations arising from this campaign, and it soon began working in conjunction with the railways to make the most of the hard-won midweek afternoon off, by offering these workers cheap worthwhile outings dovetailed into the times at which they were free. For a mere 2s 6d (12½p) return they were offered a special train from London Bridge at 12.55pm, or from East Croydon at 1.15pm, allowing six hours of Brighton breezes, not returning until 8.30pm. Curiously, the VECA did not practice what it preached by giving its own employees a midweek break to catch the 'Half-Day-Off Express'; for its own early closing day was not until Saturday. At least two other cheap midweek half-day-off trains existed, run on Wednesday and Thursday afternoons under 'Restall's Trips' patronage, again at 2s 6d return. These left Victoria on Wednesdays at 12.25 and East Croydon at 12.45; or on Thursdays at 12.45 from London Bridge, at 12.55 from New Cross, or from East Croydon at 1.10pm.

In 1929 SR at last announced its intention of electrifying the full length coastal run, and the Mayor of Brighton was formally informed of this decision by Sir Herbert Walker. Brighton was

The last Brighton 'Atlantic' to survive; *Beachy Head* splendidly turned out for a RCTS special in 1952 at Brighton. No. 32424 finished a long working career on 24 April 1958 by running empty stock from Lancing to Micheldever, and thence to Eastleigh for scrapping.
(*LCGB/Ken Nunn Collection*)

more than ready for this modernity, its boundaries having been recently extended to five times their former area. Its population was fast approaching the level of the 1931 Census, when it totalled 147,427; not counting another 54,994 residents of Hove. These numbers were swollen by tens of thousands of annual holidaymakers, and untold thousands of day excursionists, until its popular soubriquet of 'London By The Sea' was well earned. For every Sussex accent overheard in the streets, and for every polished word from the Squares, hundreds of clipped-Cockney tones overrode them with strident squawks of working class enjoyment.

The death knell of steam

The first long stage of electrification outside the suburbs, running out to Reigate and onwards to Three Bridges, was opened on 17 July 1932. In preparation for further development Haywards Heath station was rebuilt, with new subways to the platforms for coping with the increased passenger usage which was forecast. Disruption of existing services during this widespread work was expected to be minimal, from the railway's previous experience of having converted about four hundred miles of suburban track without major upheavals to passengers. Soon non-public test trains reached Brighton itself, and on 1 January 1933 a full public service opened to Brighton. As predicted, services were more frequent rather than faster, continuing at the traditional timing which inspired the Londoner's favourite if inaccurate railway slogan, 'Sixty miles in sixty minutes': the distance was actually only about fifty-one miles.

This view of the *Southern Belle* behind No. 83 near Purley was taken in about 1912. Seven cars were built for this service in 1908 weighing 40 tons each. They were the successors to the stock of the *Pullman Limited*, which were American built.

(LCGB/Ken Nunn Collection)

A superb view of the *Brighton Belle* up train leaving Patcham tunnel on 30 June 1935.

(LCGB/Ken Nunn Collection)

Above Left:
One of the 55 'Vulcans'. No. 436 was built at Newton-le-Willows in 1893, and lasted until 1952 when this picture was taken. *(P. J. Tyrrell)*

Bottom Left:
Class B2X 4-4-0 express engine No. 319 heads an up train at East Croydon in 1926. The locomotive was built in September 1896 to a design by R. J. Billinton and was orginally named *John Fowler*. It was later named *Leconfield*. There were 24 engines in this class. Railwaymen preferred the 'Gladstones' and called the new engines 'Grasshoppers' after their rough-riding characteristics. Marsh rebuilt 319 with a larger boiler as Class B2X in 1914 and Colonel Billinton fitted the top-feed dome in 1921. The locomotive was scrapped in 1930.

(LCGB/Ken Nunn Collection)

Nearly three hundred new carriages were built, from Pullmans down to slow and suburban four-car units. For express running, the SR produced six-car units, some incorporating Pullman cars.

From the end of June in 1934 the *Southern Belle* took the new name of *Brighton Belle*. Among the Pullmans for the *Brighton Belle* at least one survives today in regular service: *Audrey* which is now run on the restored *Orient Express* to the Kent Coast ports.

Laurel, Hardy and Victoria

Victoria station established a precedent in September 1933 when a News Theatre (cinema) opened on the main concourse, providing cine films and newsreels for passengers who had an hour or so on their hands. It was nearly always crammed and with a long waiting queue, for the Victoria Cartoon Cinema was among London's most popular cheap entertainments. It showed lightweight short pictures ranging from Laurel and Hardy or Charlie Chaplin to 'interest' films and Donald Duck, almost always with the current newsreels which were, for many patrons, the highlights of the show. (In 1953 a full length Coronation film was on the screen within days of the crowning of Elizabeth II, encouraging many suburbians to travel up to Victoria specially to see it in colour. Few families possessed TV, and then only in black-and-white.)

Soon both railwaymen and passengers of the 1930s had more on their minds than running everyday services, or chuckling at Chaplin in the Victoria news cinema. For the second time in the same half-century, world war loomed like a thunder cloud, to envelop the railway and the people it served in an even greater conflict than before. None of them dreamed that it would last for nearly six wearying years.

10

Run Rabbit Run

Once again war disrupted every aspect of life and commerce. The railway's main purpose as a carrier changed, from transporting commuters, excursionists and peacetime freight, into taking commuters, war workers, civil defence personnel, heavy wartime goods, and troops. The latter grew into a continuous traffic as the conflict gathered momentum, transported to the ports for embarkation or brought back wounded, or on leave. Men were also carried into rural and coastal Sussex for billeting and training in both camps and private accommodation. Railway operations came under stresses unknown in peacetime, for which even the First World War did not always provide comparable precendents.

This is London

'This is London': the fateful words reserved only for the very gravest national crises, broadcast over the radio, signalled the official outbreak of a war which over the past year had become ever more inevitable; so much so that police and other reserve personnel had already been on semi-alert, training regularly in ARP work, bomb drill and firefighting. For them the relentless progression was rammed home by the issue of gas masks and the holding of drumhead services praying that peace might yet be found, but pledging their loyalty should it not be possible.

Within days of the formal declaration the first signs of war readiness appeared on the line, as stations region-wide began to be given replacement blue bulbs instead of normal lighting, less visible from the air to the bombers which were expected at any time.

Evacuation specials were chartered by the score to take thousands of London children away from the city and suburbs. New Cross Gate bore a particularly heavy load of these departures, receiving children from the poorest and most overcrowded South-east suburban streets. They were marched to this and other stations in long two-by-two crocodiles, whole schools together, marshalled by teachers and volunteer workers. Each child clutched only one bag or case of personal belongings, and wore a regulation gasmask in its oblong cardboard box, slung round his neck on string, together with a label stating his name and school pinned to the coat. Evacuees, more than anything else, brought home to both civilians and the railwaymen who transported them that the war was real, and that it would not be

An East Croydon scene of 1926 showing a Class E5 No. 593. The old *Hollington* was built in May 1904. Engines of Class E5 were capable of 70mph on outer commuter trains. By the 1950s they were worn out and relegated to light duties such as shed pilots and short pick-up goods. (*LCGB/Ken Nunn Collection*)

over in the few weeks which had once been popularly considered sufficient for defeating Hitler.

Public train services were drastically reduced at first but – as at the outset of the previous world war – they gradually improved again as emergency timetables were consolidated into more permanent wartime working.

Holidaymaking ceased along the vulnerable South Coast, facing towards France whose fall suddenly became frighteningly possible, or even probable. Beaches and cliffs were put out of bounds to civilians, entangled with barbed wire defences, tank traps, concrete pillboxes, observation posts, and gun emplacements. The healthy south was no longer healthy, in the sense that it looked directly into the line of attack from Europe. Hotels previously able to ask a profitable 11s 6d (57½p) a night or 3 guineas (£3.15) a week for board residence lost their custom overnight; but for many it was partially offset by the boarding of military personnel who must be accommodated near the ports of Newhaven and Shoreham, or by the billeting of troops for whom existing army camps were as yet inadequate.

After Dunkirk, troop trains poured up from the coast to London, principally through the Kent ports of Dover and Folkestone, but also from Newhaven, Portsmouth, and minor Sussex and Hampshire harbours. For every train packed with weary and muddy soldiers sent on its way, enough men came in from the Little Ships to pack another two. Controlling these numberless specials, especially those crossing from Kent, fell

117

The old engine shed at Brighton in 1925, with a Class E1 0-6-0T and crew preparing to go on duty.
(*LCGB/Ken Nunn Collection*)

principally to Redhill. Redhill's speciality was changing engines in record times almost unknown before; sometimes in only four to five minutes.

'A grand crew'

Throughout the war ambulance trains brought their special quota of 'boys'. Some were bandaged and in slings or on crutches, able to catcall joyously to green old Blighty from the windows; others were on stretchers laid in former excursion compartments, too badly wounded to muster more than a thankful thumbs-up gesture. On stations where these trains halted, volunteers pushed laden trolleys along the platforms, handing up hot drinks, cigarettes, and simple comforts; a cracked mug of poor wartime-quality tea gulped on a station platform tasted better than the best banquet the imagination could devise.

One former railwayman summed up for the author the special spirit of pride and unremitting hard labour of running a wartime railway and dealing with the often harrowing cargoes of ambulance trains. The Brighton line men were 'a grand crew', doing a difficult job against almost impossible conditions.

Inspection trains took to the rails, as specials, running down from Redhill to Hastings, Lewes, Eastbourne, and Newhaven in preparation for a possible Allied invasion, carrying military commanders and strategists in the old peacetime observation saloons.

For over five years leave-trains rumbled through, taking

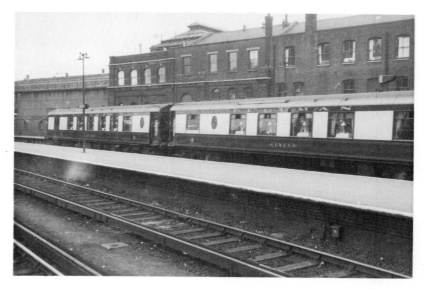

The *Brighton Belle* in Brighton Station 9 June 1963. *(D. J. Mason)*

soldiers to home leave or back to the Front in Europe. Boys in khaki packed the corridors and leaned out of the windows as they drew into towns, whistling and calling to people stopping alongside the line or on bridges to wave at them. They were play-acting at the carefree progress of a pre-war excursion special though they knew that these were no pleasure trips, and that for some of them there would be no use for a return ticket to Blighty.

The characteristic uproar of an approaching 'trooper' was unmistakable; a blended din of shouts, wolf-whistles and rough-voiced singing of current hit songs. Their repertoire steadily increased through the years, taken mainly from the radio or from troupes of British entertainers sent to play at troops' concerts overseas, and included 'Lili Marlene', 'Run Rabbit Run' and the 'Hokey-Cokey'.

Bombing on the line

The bombing of London got well under way during 1940. Victoria and London Bridge were both temporarily incapacitated; in December 1940 most of London Bridge station and its hotel were almost destroyed, to be left ramshackle and truncated for many years after the war until rebuilding in recent times. Among other early railway casualties was the Pullman car *Audrey*, built for the *Brighton Belle*, which was badly damaged during a Victoria air raid; not until 1947 was it repaired, after which it rejoined the *Belle*.

Though they escaped the torment of Dover, which was shelled from across the Channel as well as bombed, Brighton and Hove paid their own price in raids. Up to November 1941 they had undergone twenty-five air raids in which 127 people were killed; the largest number of dead among twenty-two ports and resorts from Scotland round to Falmouth when they were officially listed

The electric *Brighton Belle* as most of us best remember her. The 11.00 am prestige Victoria – Brighton train seen on 26 June 1949.

(LCGB/Ken Nunn Collection)

as coastal victims. In this same period 4,500 local houses were damaged, in addition to shops, businesses, hotels and railway targets.

Tip-and-run raids (or sneak-raids) were common here, perpetrated by just a few daring bombers, and sometimes in broad daylight, streaking in over the sea so low that defences could not be properly trained on them. In May 1943 one such raid left the Brighton station approaches littered with debris and pot holes, and two of the giant arches of Rastrick's noble viaduct destroyed; above the gap, unsupported rails balanced 70ft up in mid-air, like threads of a spider's web thrown from twig to twig. This particular bomb homed in almost horizontally, so low as to crash through a garden wall, through a house and out the other side, to explode inside the viaduct. A similar Sussex incident at St Leonards saw a bomb zooming in low enough to pass underneath seafront tram wires before demolishing the ancient church of the same name.

Repairs to the viaduct were fast, driven on by wartime urgency; in only a month temporary supports put the viaduct back into commission, while the brickwork was rebuilt.

Conventional bombs were backed up in the latter months by the sinister 'doodlebug', whose pilotless engine cut off into nerve-tingling silence moments before it crashed and exploded. Victoria fell a doodlebug victim in 1944, when seventeen people were killed on the eastern side of the station.

A typical incident recalled by one crewman perfectly recaptures the spirit of running a wartime railway: 'A goods train was making its way up the main line just when a raid was on; the

The water tank and signal box are prominent in this view taken just to the right of view 1. A standard 2-6-4T loco and 4-4-0 Schools class No. 30929 are in the shed yard. Behind them, also in steam, is one of Brighton's allocation of 'West Country' pacifics used on the inter-region trains to Cardiff and Plymouth. This is 34012 *Launceston*. (D. J. Mason)

train was going through a well known station at the time. The staff knew that the raider dropped more than the two bombs as it dived, but could only find the two craters, and then realised that a goods train was at the time passing through the station. Possibly it was on the train. They signalled forward to have the train stopped and examined, and, sure enough, they found the bomb nestling amongst some straw packing on one of the wagons.'

Attacks on the railways as a whole killed about nine hundred people, of whom nearly four hundred were railwaymen. Inevitably, the highest casualties were on the Southern, the 'Front Line Railway', with about three hundred killed. Nearly as many were lost by London Transport.

Every former railwayman has vivid memories of the blitz years: the individual incidents that collectively made up the war history of the Southern. Those serving near London Bridge saw one of the more gruesome results of bombings when, in the locality of a lost London monastery, dismembered human bones believed to have come from its plague burial ground were blown out of the earth.

Two or three ambulance trains operated out of Horley, bringing in injured men from such incidents as the Dieppe Raid

121

Steam was still used on the cross-country services to Plymouth and Cardiff. Here 'West Country' pacific No. 34100 *Appledore* leaves Brighton on 11.30am to Plymouth on 16 March 1963. (*D. J. Mason*)

for transfer to local centres, including a Canadian hospital. Unofficially, nurses were often given short footplate rides as the locomotive ran-round its train, having become friendly with the regular crews. When one train was transferred to Willesden, its departure from Horley was lengthened by about forty minutes to allow nurses and railwaymen to say goodbye to each other with a small farewell party.

One crew recalled how tanks were taken from Redhill to Worthing for practice in loading and unloading these unwieldy vehicles on a siding. Railwaymen had their own version of the reason for this: 'They always seemed to do this in the morning rush-hours; was this done to make out to the public that we had more tanks than we really had?'

Other crews were set to shunt newly crated Bren gun carriers and new Sherman tanks at Merstham, for onward conveyance to a depot at Caterham.

Ammunition trains frequently moved on this line, forming one huge potential bomb on wheels whose dangers became very apparent during an air raid. An ammunition train of fifty to sixty loaded wagons was stopped in East Croydon station during one particularly violent air raid, forming a worse threat to the town than the bombs themselves. 'If "Gerry" had hit it, I don't think there would have been anything of East Croydon left,' was the opinion of one of this train's crewmen.

Some of the signalling was still of the traditional type,

122

The *Brighton Belle* when new
c. 1932. *(Pamlin Prints)*

reminding one Brighton railwayman of an ingenious little makeshift adopted on this line, enabling crews waiting at signals to relax instead of fixedly watching for the signal arm to move. Onto the end of the lower-quadrant type of semaphore signal, the train fireman would hang by its handle an old tin or zinc bucket from the cab. When the arm 'came off' the bucket would automatically fall to the ground, with a loud enough rattle to alert the engine crew. This ploy was especially favoured by shunter crews, apt to be held for lengthy periods at the siding signals.

Brighton Works' wartime peak of locomotive production rapidly declined with the approaching end of Southern steam, and they were abandoned by BR for engine building in 1958. Eventually BR demolished the historic buildings which had produced Brighton and Southern steam locomotives for over a hundred years since May 1852.

Return of peace

Services began to pick up after the war ended in 1945, but the resumed upsurge of cheap family motoring saw to it that rail excursion traffic would never regain the massed madness of the Twenties and Thirties. Through specials from the North and Midlands declined, and in London individual day return tickets by scheduled trains tended to displace the former ultra-cheap half-crown specials to Brighton.

123

Class N 2-6-0 No. 31844 at Brighton shed in 1949 minus front pair of driving wheels. This locomotive had been assembled at Ashford from parts manufactured by the Woolwich Arsenal and a boiler from the North British Loco. Co. in September 1924. It was withdrawn in January 1964. The first N came out on 27th July 1917 and was the freight version of the Class K No. 790. They both had the same boilers. The class eventually totalled 80 engines and served successfully all over the Southern. No. 31874 is preserved on the Mid-Hants Railway. (*P. J. Tyrrell*)

The *Belle* came back into its own, a solitary bastion of elegance in an unglamorous and war weary world where the austerity regime still cast its greyness over many aspects of life. In her first job, the author once invested the normal fare plus a 5s (25p) Pullman supplement for one glimpse into this other world of luxury train travel which by then was as much a legend as a timetabled fact. It bought memories for a lifetime: of dark inlaid panelling, exquisite marquetry, seats as sumptuous as thrones, brass table lamps with pink shades, and wheels running as smooth as silk. One never forgot a journey on the *Belle*; even if one could not afford the double Pullman supplement and was forced to be content with a return by ordinary train.

The South Croydon disaster

Periodically the Brighton line of the Southern Railway endured its share of accidents, though nothing like so frequently as in the early decades. The worst of these happened only weeks before the Southern ceased to exist on being merged into British Railways, when at South Croydon thirty-one people died in the early morning of 24 October 1947. Two trains, both on the 'up' main line, collided in thick fog – a killer on a scale unknown today which was the main cause of many a railway accident or near miss, of which this and the famous Ilford crash were among the more spectacular.

The 7.33am Haywards Heath to London Bridge and the 8.04am Tattenham Corner to London Bridge train met as the Haywards Heath train slowed near South Croydon, to be rammed hard in the rear by the Tattenham Corner service, approaching too

A Southern Railway holiday brochure of about 1937, sold at station bookstalls. (*Ward Lock Ltd*)

fast for the extremely limited visibility. Both were crowded with commuters and schoolchildren. The leading pair of Tattenham Corner coaches were telescoped and wrenched off their bogies, and their roofs torn off; the last pair of the Haywards Heath carriages were derailed, flung aside until one of them precariously overhung a steep drop to a road. Over thirty passengers and crew died.

Residents living near the line were quickly on the scene, welcoming injured passengers into their homes until ambulances

125

An old sign in Southern Green survives on the approach to Brighton. (*M. V. Searle*)

could collect them. As in the comparable Lewisham crash, also in a built-up area, they proved themselves as unstinting as the official rescue services, unsparingly tearing up sheets and table-cloths for emergency bandages, comforting the victims, and brewing cups of strong tea. Their service continued for many hours to sustain the breakdown gangs drafted into the scene, handing tea and sandwiches over the fences to these tired men. Only those dwelling permanently beside a main line, such as the present author, have to live with the background fear of a crash at the ends of their gardens; some even keep supplies of bandages and simple medicines in the house for this very eventuality.

Fog made the Croydon rescue work and clearance of the wreckage doubly difficult, and eerily magnified the cries of the injured from inside the grotesque piles of twisted debris, wrapping clammy grey fingers of vapour around everything and reducing visibility to mere yards. It was a direct ancestor of the Great Smog of only five years later, which changed the course of legislation, so widespread were its effects.

The great smog of 1952

When winter fog was thickened by emissions from factory chimneys, domestic coal fires, and by steam locomotives, mingling with natural heavy mists off the Thames and hanging in almost motionless air, the deadly combination of London smog (smoke plus fog) was produced. It stood before the eyes like a thick blanket of rancid yellowish-green-grey cobweb, so impenetrable that visibility was reduced to only a few groping feet. Smog was a killer of chest and lung sufferers, and a strangulator of traffic and commerce. Its climax was reached in the Great Smog of 1952, which brought the whole of London and its suburbs to a semi-standstill for two or three days on end. If they moved at all,

126

16 March 1962 and No. 468 now awaits its end out in the open in Hove goods yard. The connecting rods are laid across the buffer beam, and the 75A shed code has been removed. *(D. J. Mason)*

trains were as choked with vapours inside the compartments as outside, let in with every opening of the doors. Signals were invisible to drivers, who had to depend only on fog-signals (detonators) placed on the track to explode loudly under the wheels as a guide to the driver's whereabouts, as he crawled along. Flares spluttered and hissed on road islands and outside station yards to guide floundering pedestrians; large black kettle-like containers from whose long skinny spouts bright flames spumed as identifying landmarks in the gloom; but the chances of catching a train when one reached the platforms were unpredictable. Many trains did grope through, but timetables were non-existent, and waiting time was long.

The Great Smog brought London to a halt in a way that all Hitler's bombs had failed to achieve. It killed, directly or indirectly, some four hundred people, and resulted in the Clean Air Acts which forbade smog-making coal fires and furnaces, until even common fog became comparatively rare, as it is today.

Other, if less severe, natural problems of railway operation are still with us, notably the annual deposition of wet autumn leaves on the rails. Today, electric trains stall and slither on them as they become compacted into slimy grease.

Yesterday the problem was much the same; the mouth of Clayton tunnel is specially recalled among railwaymen as a ready-made receptacle for falling leaves, piled so thickly at the entrance that wheels merely spun on the spot, unable to move forward.

Nationalisation

1923 brought in the first major nationwide amalgamation of railways, into the Big Four. Twenty-five years later they, in turn, disappeared into one universal system divided into regions, when British Railways came into being on 1 January 1948.

127

Brighton Station c. 1982/3.
(*M. V. Searle*)

Geographically, the Southern was among the least disturbed parts, forming in the main the new Southern Region.

In 1952 the Brighton works at Preston Park undertook the restoration of Pullman cars for the revived *Golden Arrow* boat-train to Dover and Folkestone. Among these was *Phoenix*, appropriately so renamed after being revived from the ashes of the former *Rainbow*, which had been burned out back in 1936. When Brighton had finished with *Rainbow/Phoenix* it looked as luxurious as ever.

The Coronation

Elizabeth II's coronation in 1953 put the same pressures onto the railways as did previous royal occasions, bringing tens of thousands of spectators to London to see the processions and decorations, even though the weather forecast of 'Real Queen's weather' turned out to be very wrong and very wet. Main termini were decorated and some were floodlit. Over sixty specials carried in thirty thousand servicemen for lining the route to Westminster Abbey, with three thousand extra police, and thousands of schoolchildren. In the suburbs normal train services ended around midnight, and special trains to London took over from about one o'clock in the morning, keeping staff and rolling stock on twenty-four-hour alert; one person's day out was always another's hard work.

Another big rail strike disrupted the Southern Region in 1955. Ironically, it was 'outdated' steam that came to the rescue as electric trains almost disappeared off the rails, temporarily

During the last war, Raworth and Bulleid introduced electric locos for the Southern Railway. The first one, No. 200001, passes Hove with a goods train on 27 July 1963. Only three of these were built. They could pick up power from third rail or overhead supply, and they had a flywheel driven generator to maintain power over breaks in the third rail. This loco was not withdrawn until 1 January 1969. (*D. F. Mason*)

bringing in such unexpected visitors as the *West Country* Pacifics. The commuter's nightmare was the train spotter's dream.

From Racecourse to Airport

Gatwick Airport began to expand as early as the 1950s with the new fashion for foreign holidays, as air travel came down in price to ordinary travellers' levels. Neither the airport nor its station were adequate for this new generation of holidaymakers. The existing Gatwick Airport station closed down (now visible only as a neglected grassgrown platform), and a new modern station was opened a little to the north, on the site of the former Gatwick Racecourse station. Today the main runways can be seen from passing trains, as jets scream into take-off and landing, low over the roofs of the carriages. Milling crowds almost continually throng the platforms, both by day and by night; for all-night trains serve this station from Victoria. Well groomed pilots and stewardesses wait in uniform among the tired and dishevelled holidaymakers constantly coming and going by train, fed directly to the platforms by covered walkways from the customs halls. Gatwick demonstrates how closely air and rail travel can be integrated, to the benefit of both.

If steam trains serving the seaside symbolised the Brighton line before the two world wars, Gatwick came to embody the electric train age and the post-war period. It links Victoria and Brighton with cities all over the world by the comparatively simple expedient of stepping off a train directly into an international airport.

11

End of the 'Belle' Epoch

Holidaymaking requirements changed dramatically during the 1960s and 1970s, taking away the century-old emphasis on British seaside reorts in favour of places as far afield as an airliner can fly at charter fares. Even day tripping has expanded geographically, with the growth of motorways. Brighton beach, more than good enough for our grandparents and great-grandparents, now has to compete with the Costas for only a part share in the travel trade. The family car became universal after the Second World War, taking its owners not only on day outings but also on holiday. During their vacation, it was to the car that people turned for pleasure jaunts around the resort, rather than to trains.

Nor was the upper-crust section of the market unaffected by changes in taste, as the decline of the *Brighton Belle* confirmed.

Last days of the Brighton Belle

By the Sixties the *Brighton Belle* was becoming an anachronism: a last outpost of dated luxury travel harking back to the high society life of Brighton which had begun with the Royal Pavilion, the big houses of the Squares, and the patronage of society. It was also a last outpost of the era of named trains, whose titles automatically suggested extra sumptuousness of accommodation and decoration, or an extra turn of non-stop speed, and usually both.

Except for the war years, this train had run almost continuously since the 1890s under various guises, including the *Sunday Pullman Limited* (1898), the *Southern Belle* (1908), and the *Brighton Belle* (1934). In imitation of the *Orient Express* it was popularly given a small veneer of intrigue to overlay its perfect respectability, in the tales that prevailed of 1930s race-gangs patronising the train, plotting their little crimes on the move where they were unlikely to be overheard.

One of the *Belle*'s famous features was in its full meal service, with a train staff said to total sixty people working almost entirely in the culinary and service aspects. But by the 1960s demand for full meals had slumped as public taste – and pockets – veered away from big eating towards lighter snacks and coffees. Its famous kipper breakfasts were banished from the menu in 1969, but to such a howl of protest, led by the actor who is now Lord Olivier, that they were soon restored; kippers were still being served on the final day's runs, at a mere 22p a pair.

The coaches, like the kippers, had seen better days and were considered to be on their last legs in their current form; they fell

A line of unwanted steam engines at Hove awaiting the final journey to the cutter's torch. 30901 is a 'Schools' Class locomotive which was named *Winchester*. (*D. J. Mason*)

short of modern safety and timekeeping standards unless heavy expenditure was to be invested in restoration.

The very suggestion that the *Brighton Belle* was doomed created vociferous protests from those who could afford to value it as a reminder of elegance in an increasingly harsh world. Again, the outcry was led by Olivier, a distinguished Brighton resident and regular user of the train. But in vain; the last runs were announced, making the threat a certainty.

The official final trip was a £10-a-head champagne farewell, following the day's other scheduled services, carrying between them over a thousand sentimental passengers. Some travelled wearing Edwardian period costume; others sported 1920s boaters and blazers, bringing back the spirit of an age that was dying with every click of the wheels; the spirit which, according to hearsay, had once pampered passengers with real silver teapots, luxurious footstools, and upholstery fit for a throne.

The *Belle* was special and unique; a flash of sunshine gold swishing through with that subdued toy-train wheel rhythm of the classic Pullman car. We who regarded it as one of the happier facts of life, from frequent glimpses as it shot on its way south of Croydon, felt that the line was suddenly emptier, however heavily populated it might be with ordinary suburban units.

Briefly, in about 1964/65, another named train was tried out, the *Regency Belle*; merely a *Brighton Belle* set under commercial guise. This was only an evening departure, for expensive wining and dining at Brighton followed by nightclubbing and gambling, and a breakfast-trip back to London in the very small hour of 2 o'clock in the morning. It was not a financial success, and lasted only a few weeks.

Even the more ordinary kind of Pullman car, set in the centre of a standard main line unit, had its special air of distinction, rarely disturbed by such an incident as was recounted by one

131

The Beeching Axe fell on the Shoreham-Steyning-Horsham, line in 1966. In the last few months 3-car diesel units operated, but on 19 April 1963, Class 2 tank (The Mickeys) No. 41301 heads the 4.35pm to Horsham. Photographed at Hove passing a 2-Hal electric units on the Portsmouth to Brighton stopping service. *(D. J. Mason)*

guard from the latter days of Pullman working: 'A pal of mine was working a twelve-car train non-stop; it came to a halt with its front well past the signal, in a tunnel. The guard, realising something was wrong, started off to meet the driver, who would be walking down the offside to meet him; . . . they found that a train line between two coaches had come apart, but not fallen. After replacing it, they made their respective ways back. As the guard passed the Pullman car, the attendant called out: 'Guard: I have a drunk in here, he is causing a disturbance; can I bring him back to you?' The guard, obviously not feeling the ticket, realising all the explaining he had to do about the delay, answered rather sharply: 'You got him drunk. Now you get him sober!'

£32 a quarter

The most rapid modern changes on the line were in fares, continually rising in tune with the rocketing cost of living. 1967 provides an example of travel costs that, even by the Seventies, were already old-fashioned. A man could then commute from a new £10,000 house on the Brighton outskirts, or an older £2,600 cottage in the back streets, with a £32. 17s (£32.85) quarterly season ticket to London, or take a Second Class single for just 14s (70p), or an off-peak day return for 15s 9d (79p). Other

132

End of the line for two Brighton stalwarts, E6 32418 and Class K, No. 32338. Surely if ever there was a class that deserved to have a representative preserved it was Lawson Billinton's mogul Class K, for they were among the finest Brighton locos ever produced.

(D. J. Mason)

comparable costs were £26. 18s (£26.90), for a Three Bridges to London quarterly season, or a mere £13. 10s (£13.50) for one from East Croydon to London. By the fastest train, at fifty-three minutes, Brighton could be reached from Croydon off-peak for only 12s 3d (61p) return, or Eastbourne for just 16s 9d (84½p). As for the local run from Preston Park to Lewes (21min): the old fare of 3s 6d (17½p) began to read like fiction.

The Preservation Movement

Even on those lines which still were not fully electrified, notably that to Bournemouth, steam was rapidly dying during the mid-Sixties. On the Brighton line electric traction had by then been in the ascendant for three decades. Yet many ex-Brighton steam locomotives were determined to survive, being great favourites of the preservation movement for their attractive character: above all, the perky little 'Terriers' which can be found on many a private steam railway today. They include No. 46 *Newington* (*Freshwater*), whose many vicissitudes included a stint in the guise of *The Hayling Billy* displayed outside a public house of that name, before ending its days on the Isle of Wight. Also on the Island is No. 40 *Brighton* (renamed as No. 11, *Newport*).

Another 'Terrier', *Knowle*, was acquired by the West Somerset Railway, after a spell on static display at Butlin's nearby

133

Opposite top:
Cathay Pacific airliner taking off over a rapid city link train at Gatwick. (*M. V. Searle*)

Aircraft constantly land and take off over the Gatwick station platforms. (*M. V. Searle*)

One of the pre-'Gatwick Express' Airport electric multiple units waits at the airport. (*M. V. Searle*)

Opposite bottom:
No. 47-248 on through Inter-City train at Gatwick Airport Station in August 1983. The attitude of railway staff to the photographer has changed since our Victorian forefathers. They would have posed in great numbers before the camera, unlike their modern-day counterparts, who seem a trifle bored by any attention paid to them. (*M. V. Searle*)

Minehead Holiday Camp. Two more went to the Kent and East
Sussex Railway under the present names of *Bodiam* and *Sutton*.

The marvellous steam museum at Bressingham in Norfolk has
the ex-Brighton *Martello*, another Stroudley locomotive, also
taken from one of Butlin's camps; she was repainted at
Bressingham in her old 'Marsh umber' livery. To the Bluebell
Railway went the popular pair of O-6-OT AIXs, *Stepney* and
Fenchurch, both dating from the 1870s; the latter was paraded at
the spectacular Shildon cavalcade marking the 150th anniversary
of steam passenger carrying railways in 1975. The two KESR
engines have been undergoing boiler repairs; *Sutton*, having
had her boiler returned and her motion overhauled, was operational again for the summer of 1984. *Bodiam* was expected to be
back in traffic in the late summer of 1986, restored to her BR
number (32670) and to BR livery.

The expansion of Gatwick

Gatwick Airport and station rapidly developed during the 1960s.
Later a Rapid City Link electric service joined the airport to
London, and some passengers could save further time by checking-
in in advance at Victoria, including those booked with British
Caledonian. Escalators and stairs at Gatwick station carried them
directly into the departure and customs hall and returned them
to the platforms on the homeward journey. The Rapid City Link
train journey was timed for only forty-two minutes. It ran hourly
all night, and four times an hour through most of the daylight
and evening hours.

Joint rail/air terminal halls were added to Victoria station at an
upper level above the platforms in 1962, approached by
escalators from the concourse. The Surrey and Sussex aviation
world had certainly come a long way since the informal pre-war

During the last war, Raworth and Bulleid introduced electric locos for the Southern Railway. The first one, No. 20001, passes Hove with a goods train on 27 July 1963. Only three of these were built. They could pick up power from third rail or overhead supply, and they had a flywheel driven generator to maintain power over breaks in the third rail. This loco was not withdrawn until 1 January 1969. *(D. J. Mason)*

period when aircraft were recognisable by name as they flew low into the then very important Croydon Aerodrome, above the roofs of passing steam trains: *Scylla* and *Scipio*, *Heracles* and *Hercules*, and other gods of the pioneer skies.

Electric working in the 1960s

Railway working, too, had greatly progressed, based on practicality and not on yesterday's impossible dream of a 100mph electric train linking London and Brighton alone (without any intermediate stations) to almost fly Londoners to the sea, and seaside commuters to the City.

As well as resulting in new rolling stock, full electric working brought in new tasks, and new tools for doing them. Some turned out to have various non-railway uses, as one former guard recalled: 'A few women are very difficult indeed, for instance the ones who will wear high heels when travelling. They very often lose a shoe while boarding a train, and it is usually the guard who retrieves it for them, off the track, using a tool which is very useful for this task, but is on the train for another more important function. It happens to be hooked at one end which is handy for putting in the handle of a handbag or in a shoe to lift it up, so that it can be taken hold of, which saves time and risk of injury getting onto the track. This causes delay that is not easily explained, or made up on the journey.' The useful handbag and

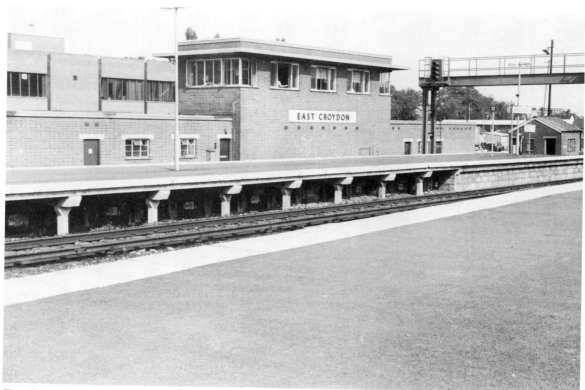

East Croydon signal box. (*M. V. Searle*)

East Croydon on the electrified main Brighton line. (*M. V. Searle*)

Class 73 No. 73125 waits at East Croydon with bulk freight train. *(M. V. Searle)*

47122 on down freight train at East Croydon August 1983. *(M. V. Searle)*

The traditional railway company canopy, as demonstrated at Brighton. *(M. V. Searle)*

No. 09020 shunts an empty special out of Brighton terminus. August 1983. *(M. V. Searle)*

Brighton approaches as seen in
August 1983. (*M. V. Searle*)

Enthusiasts wait for action at
the extremity of the Brighton
platforms in August 1983.
Note the completely isolated
signal box: only the shadow of
Mr. Craven's old offices can be
seen on its walls. (*M. V. Searle*)

shoe fishing rod was intended for switching off power at various points on the line in accident or emergency; for example, when stranded passengers must walk alongside the live rail to safety.

One gets the impression that railway suicides increased with full electrification, but the logical explanation was that it encouraged great increases in the sizes of lineside towns and new housing estates, with a resultant increase in the population. They put one of the most unpleasant duties onto train crews, as was recounted to the writer by an ex-railwayman who had seen his full share of such happenings: 'It is unfortunately a fact that a number of people, for some reason or other, choose death by throwing themselves under a train. This may or may not be a pleasant way to go, but it is not for those who have to sort it out afterwards. For instance, the driver, when it is at his end, never forgets, and the person who collects the pieces doesn't either. A guard does not see as much at his end, but sometimes he does.

. . . First one must see if there is any life in the person, and if it is possible to move them off the lines to do so, and give them first aid if needed. Should they be dead, which is most often the case, inform (by means of the nearest phone on the line) the signalman, who reports it to the police. After covering the body, you proceed on your journey and, at the end, report fully in writing . . . for the rest of the journey . . . writing a full report and doing my job, and about a fortnight later attending a court of enquiry into the incident.' Every railwayman dreads seeing a suicide, and so do people living alongside the line; the author has encountered two in a short space of recent time.

The African Chief

The commuter army swelled and swelled after the Second World War as more new towns sprang up alongside the main line, encouraged by the swift travelling to London brought about by electrification. More than ever, the classic tale of a puzzled African Chief taking his first glimpse of Victoria station rang true. Never having seen London until the age of sixty, Victoria came as a shock to the African; as the story was retold to the author by an old Brighton railwayman who, in turn, had heard it somewhere along the line: 'A friend called on him to welcome him, and found him a very frightened man. He found out from him with great difficulty that he had gone for a walk, having arrived earlier than he expected in the city, finding himself in Victoria station, in the morning rush hour, standing at one of the barriers watching a train come in. A very frightening thing happened to him there. As the train drew nearer, all the doors swung outwards and, while the train was still in motion, a great many men jumped out, quite silently, and they began to run towards him. "They carried umbrellas like spears," he said, "and their faces were set and unsmiling. I thought something terrible was about to happen."'

Rush-hour madness had, of course, its sane and logical

The never-ending bustle of Victoria (Brighton side concourse), busy even on a Sunday afternoon.

(*M. V. Searle*)

explanation but, like frogs in a moving guards van, was at first sight a puzzle. The latter incident again occurred in the rush hour, on the evening return run to the South Coast and Littlehampton. We cannot better the description of the guard concerned: 'Six boxes about two feet square were put into my brake, at the start, and along came two chaps who asked if they could ride in the brake, if it was possible for them to do so, as long as they did not sit on the parcels in the brake. A little way on the journey, one of them came to my compartment; he was very excited and informed me that the brake was alive with frogs; he said they were jumping about all over the floor. We set to and eventually caught them . . . then we saw the boxes had been placed on top of one another, so the bottom one, which was taking the weight of the other five, had split open at one corner. It was easy for them to slither out, but not so easy to put them back.' Why crates of live frogs should be riding on a Southern Region commuter train in the rush hour appears to be unexplained.

Signs of the past

A surprising number of reminders of the past still survive on the Brighton line, many of them known only to railwaymen, such as arches underneath the London viaducts which were once tiny homes for early railway staff.

At least two fragments exist where the Atmospheric Railway

Even on Sundays, Clapham
Junction is alive with trains.
(*M. V. Searle*)

Class 73 running light near
Clapham Junction, August
1983. (*M. V. Searle*)

The 1905 frontage of Earlswood station as seen on 2nd September 1984.

(David Mason)

A Sunday morning Gatwick Shuttle service train hauled by No. 73-114 passes Earlswood just south of Redhill. Only two platforms are used now. Platform 3 is fenced off on the right, and the subway to Platform 4 has been bricked up to prohibit access. Viewed on 2nd September 1984. Earlswood is treated as an unstaffed halt for stopping trains between Brighton and Victoria on Sundays.

(David Mason)

once ran. At the Brighton end of Sydenham station is said to be situated a small building with an estate agent's office overhead: formerly a pumping station for the 'Atmospheric'. In the 'up' side yard of West Croydon old railwaymen point out a wall holding up an embankment which they say is 'made completely of the concrete or stone blocks which carried the Atmospheric Railway.' It is said that marks where the chairs of the Atmospheric went into the holes in the blocks are still visible.

Until recent years an enthusiast living near the line at Purley Oaks supposedly kept in his back garden (as part of a miniature railway layout) the actual signal which was the principal cause of an accident at Stoat's Nest, later known as Coulsdon North. One old foreman recalled that this station was for one single day named Coulsdon West, until it was pointed out how incorrect, geographically, it was. Hurriedly the station signs and name boards were changed to the new name.

The terrain of the Quarry Line from Coulsdon southwards is rich in fuller's earth, once much used by biscuit manufacturers to prevent fresh biscuits sticking to one another. It was widely exported, taken by rail to Redhill in paper sacks. This unstable countryside was always inclined to embankment landslips, inspiring the railway to adopt an ingenious method of planting it with stabilising grass. As a railwayman from this area told the author: 'A coarse net like a football goal net was put over the chalk near a tunnel and impregnated with grass seed. The net was laid over the chalk until the grass took root to protect the bank from chalk falls.'

Two reminders of the Clayton Tunnel disaster are known to

About noon on 16 March 1963, Brighton Station appears almost empty. Only a Hastings via Lewes electric unit and the steam train for Horsham, behind a 'Mickey' tank, are visible. The 1882 station has little changed in appearance. (*D. J. Mason*)

ex-Southern train crews. One is a staff house built over the tunnel entrance, believed to be still in use. The other was the old Clayton Tunnel signal box, removed in about 1978 or 1979. Until then its official log was said to be kept in the box, showing among its entries the log of the famous tunnel disaster.

Half a century of electrification

The fiftieth anniversary of Brighton line electrification was celebrated on 16 July 1983 with an exhibition held on two platforms at Brighton station. It included electric unit No. 4732 (one of only a handful of old 4-SUB units still running). For the occasion it was repainted in the vivid livery colour of the Southern Railway: a brilliant malachite green with yellow lettering. This train was also glimpsed briefly during this period on such suburban lines as that from Beckenham Junction to Crystal Palace, to the surprise of commuters aboard standard BR blue suburban trains. Also on show at Brighton was a 1951 unit: the Pullman car *Audrey* (normally rostered to the restored *Orient Express* out of Victoria to the Kent ports): and a general manager's saloon made from a former Hastings line diesel-unit buffet car; this coach had already made modern railway history, by taking the Prince and Princess of Wales on their honeymoon journey to Broadlands, and the Pope from Gatwick Airport to Victoria. The electro-diesel 73142, *Broadlands*, named after the Mountbatten mansion at Romsey, attracted long queues of visitors hoping for cab visits, whilst a class 09 diesel shunter gave tantalisingly brief cab rides the length of the platform. The

147

The 'Leader' Class locomotive No. 36001 in 1950 in workshop grey. Designed by the great innovator Oliver Bulleid, Brighton's hush-hush locomotive reached only as far as Crowborough on test runs in 1948. The two other engines were never completed. British Rail was not keen on fancy designs and broke them up as quickly as possible. The trial run was very hot for the fireman who was stuck in a tiny compartment in the middle of the loco, but nice and cool for the driver who just swapped his cab at one end for the other on the return journey. Oil firing would have solved the fireman's problem, but Bulleid had resigned upon nationalisation and gone to Ireland, so no futher developments occurred on the 'Leader'. (*P. J. Tyrrell*)

moderate £1 exhibition charge also covered an open day at the rolling stock maintenance depot, made accessible to the public by a shuttle service. Specimens of BR classes 33, 47 and 56 were on show, but the greatest attraction proved to be a non-BR interloper: *Sarah Siddons*, a red electric locomotive from London Transport, sixty-three years old and specially modified to travel under her own power over the third-rail system down to Brighton.

This major one-day event, opened by the Mayor of Brighton, raised a considerable sum for the same railway charity that benefited long before by the *Gladstone* exhibition: the Southern Region children's and old folks' centre at Woking.

Electrification memories

The half-century of electrification was a time for looking backward as well as forward, as men who had driven the first 'engineless' trains resurrected their memories of the early days. Some pointed out how, if one knows where to look alongside the track, it is still possible to identify the stumps of the gantries holding the early overhead wires, about twenty yards apart. They were so closely spaced that one driver described the cab view as 'like going through a tunnel'. The main supports were 'made to last', in appearance more like signal gantries.

One former driver told the author how, at first, the

No. 33203 halted on goods train at Redhill station.
(*M. V. Searle*)

Locomotive Department 'wanted nothing to do with electrification': not because it opposed progress, but because electric trains might result in some crews losing money. The short-term solution was to train guards to be motormen, for whose benefit diamond-shaped markings were put alongside the track showing them where to shut off power: 'you did not then require much brain to stop the train.' These diamonds can still be spotted today in some places. Next the Locomotive Department agreed to work electric trains by offering men one out of every two Sundays 'on' to cover any loss of wages. This was accepted, but several ex-guards also remained in the driver's cab.

Staff relationships appear to have been exceptionally good at this early electric period. It was possible to see the management without difficulty, to iron out problems at the outset. The Pay Clerk of the time, one Mr Madge, was in particular 'a very fair man if you had wages trouble'. He was so popular that on his retirement the Brighton motormen staged a whip-round which collected several hundred pounds.

Duties were so regular and stereotyped that a man could plan his private life for weeks ahead. 'One guard, Mr Stanniford, did all the working out of turns and you never got altered on your regular job,' explained one of these crews: 'You could tell in three years' time whether you would be on at Christmas or not.'

The men's main dislike was the physical aspect of driving an early electric train, for they were not noted for crew comfort. One variety was nicknamed the 'Nelson Stock' because, like the

149

A Victoria semi-fast passes
Platform 1 at Earlswood on
Sunday 2nd September 1984.
The spacious covered area was
deemed necessary for the
protection of patients and
visitors to the nearby hospitals.
(David Mason)

Salfords station built to serve a
local factory near Horley has
perhaps the meanest station
buildings on the whole line. A
wide belt of shrubs and bushes
separates the fast lines from the
slow. The fast lines have never
received platforms at Salfords.
Photographed on Sunday 2nd
September 1984. *(David Mason)*

Horley was rebuilt in 1905 for
the widening of the lines, and
the building straddles the
tracks which run under the
roadway. On the far wall is
engraved in the stonework a
handsome monogram, with the
letters L B S C R intertwined.
On Sunday 2nd September
1984, the station was in the
throes of rebuilding again. The
front canopy has been removed
and the platform offices have
been knocked down into piles
of rubble. *(David Mason)*

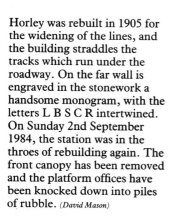

150

Trains pass the lonely Balcombe. Once through the great tunnel and over the viaduct the two tracks continue to Haywards Heath. Like other small stations on the Brighton Line, Balcombe is an unstaffed halt on Sundays. *(David Mason)*

The deserted Balcombe station, in need of painting and modernising. The footbridge leads up to the path which exits on the road high above the station. This view was taken on Sunday 2nd September 1984. Soon afterwards a stopping train to Brighton deposited the Sunday papers on the platform. They were duly collected by the local newsagent. The only sign of life that morning. It is a different matter on a weekday, as Balcombe has been extended to take 12 car trains which now stop and pick up City commuters. *(David Mason)*

Haywards Heath looking north from the enormous car-park. This station handles hundreds of commuters every week day, and on Sunday is host to many visitors who sample the delights of the Open Market. Note the 70 mph speed restriction through the station and the old signal box on the far side next to platform one. *(David Mason)*

Admiral, the trains had only limited vision. The view ahead was limited compared with the view from most trains. Also, they were susceptible to extremes of heat and cold in the cab. In winter the unheated cab could be so cold that the driver put his feet inside his tool bag to keep them warm, and his little round seat was so comfortless as to become a torment to the anatomy during a long turn of duty. After working for three or four hours, the cab would heat up, again to an extreme degree, because of the resistances sited behind the driver; it was alleged that temperatures inside the cab on a hot day, aggravated by the electrical installations, could climb over the 100° mark.

Operation New Look

Much new signalling was completed in the early to mid-1950s, and a second phase from the early 1970s, embracing work for London Bridge. Another elaborate resignalling scheme, this time for Victoria and the Brighton run, was made public in 1976 and, at the time of writing, is on the way towards completion.*

1983, the fiftieth anniversary year of Brighton line electrification, seemed an appropriate time to consider the future, whilst embarking on one of the biggest Southern Region improvement schemes of recent decades: the £120-million 'Operation New Look'. The ultimate objective was total resignalling from London to Brighton, replacement of large sections of the permanent way, and complete new layouts for Croydon.

A new Victoria Signalling Centre was completed by mid-1983, seconded by another at Three Bridges. Between them, they were designed to control the territory formerly governed by numerous individual signal boxes. The new track layout north of Croydon was a very complex undertaking, where new lines were made to fly over older ones and the criss-crossing points and crossovers were considerably simplified to divide off slow tracks from fast, to the benefit of both. This Croydon operation involved redesigning the approach roads and the construction of new bridges, cuttings and embankments for separating the individual tracks. Coal mine waste and spoil from the Betteshanger colliery in Kent was conveyed by freight train in thousands of tons, for building these massive new works.

Coulsdon North station, a bottleneck with its tangles of interweaving fast and slow lines, was eliminated. Its passengers were transferred to the very nearby Smitham. By this move BR could realign the fast main line to push express services straight through to Croydon. The Gloucester Road Triangle would thereby be simplified in the number of lines involved, able to support more intensive traffic.

On 3 July 1983 the second Signalling Centre at Three Bridges

(*still applies, March 1986)

became operational, intended eventually to speed up Brighton line running by controlling the southern part of the route, linked to the area controlled by the Victoria centre. These two Centres were intended, when in full use, to replace no fewer than seventy conventional signal boxes. The area controlled from Three Bridges was to extend from there to Coulsdon, and down to Preston Park and Brighton, also westwards along the coast to Portslade, and to Lewes.

The public was expected to notice improvements by mid-1984, well before total completion of this ambitious re-signalling scheme.

One of the more individual touches to Operation New Look was the naming of a modern class 73 locomotive as *Croydon*. On 15 September 1983 the Mayor of Croydon performed the naming ceremony at East Croydon station.

The 'Gatwick Express'

One of the greatest annoyances to ordinary Brighton line passengers has long been the ever larger heaps of luggage piled into the aisles and corridors of the trains at Gatwick Airport, and even onto the seats. The general overcrowding at this point has spoiled many a journey up from Brighton which has started in reasonably normal comfort. This problem was tackled during Operation New Look, with the announcement that from 14 May 1984 onwards a new non-stop 'Gatwick Express' Rail-Air train would run to and from Victoria, exclusively for airline passengers, thus relieving the frustration and congestion experienced by other travellers. This 'luxury service' was to take only thirty minutes on the journey, running every 15 minutes.

Between 14 May and 31 December of 1984, about 2,300,000 passengers joined the handsome-looking 'Gatwick Express' units, a rise of 31.7% over figures of the previous year, paying over £7,000,000 into the ticket offices.

Where once rail and horse-drawn coach combined to give Londoners a faster journey than ever before to Brighton, rail and air now unite in carrying the development process towards the twenty-first century. The destination is not only Brighton, but also the ends of the earth.

One speculates that Rennie and Rastrick, Cundy and Stephenson, and all those others whose dream was a railway to Brighton which would travel faster than any horse could gallop, might have approved the line's present march of speed and progress.

All bustle at Haywards Heath station frontage on Sunday 2nd September 1984. People are making their way to and from the Open Market which is just under the railway bridge on the right. *(David Mason)*

Speed is restricted to 40 mph through the short tunnel at the south end of Haywards Heath station yard. Unit 7721 is about to enter the portals with a slow train to Brighton. Concrete sleepers for relaying the track are stacked in the foreground. (2/9/84.) *(David Mason)*

The end of Wivelsfield platform looking south towards Keymer Junction. Unit 7433 heads a semi-fast to Victoria. There are cross-overs either side of this station so that wrong line working is possible during track maintenance or in case of accident. The signal on the left (T369) shows the left hand fork split for Lewes and Eastbourne, and the right for Brighton and Worthing. On the right, T371, the indications are for Lewes and the upper split for regaining the correct line at the southern cross-over. Note the 12 car stop sign for wrong-line working. *(David Mason)*

154

Extra bus shelters have been erected on Wivelsfield platforms, due to increased numbers of users from the expanding suburbs of Burgess Hill, Wivelsfield, and the quaintly named World's End. Unit 7797 heads the 15.52 stopping train to Brighton on Sunday 2nd September, 1984.

(David Mason)

Keymer Junction on 2nd September 1984. The lines curving to the left are for Lewes and straight ahead for Clayton Tunnel and Brighton. The fire which has devastated the foliage of the railway bank on the right, had spread far enough to engulf an apple tree. Not a leaf was left, but a profusion of baked apples hung from the blackened boughs.

(David Mason)

Like Horley, Burgess Hill station offices are on an overbridge. The old station house on the left is boarded up, but the garden is still tended. This view, looking north towards Wivelsfield was taken on 2nd September 1984.

(David Mason)

Hassocks was rebuilt in the Seventies. The bus shelters have replaced the wide station canopies and the neat station house, but the traveller can stilll view the old buildings as a mural has been placed on the ticket-office and waiting room wall depicting the front elevation of the old 1887 station. (2/9/84) *(David Mason)*

The connecting bus service outside Hassocks station on 2nd September 1984. *(David Mason)*

Hassocks survivor. The old signal box is still used as a ground frame, but is not staffed. Unit 7361 heads the 16.43 slow to Victoria past the box on Sunday 2nd September 1984. *(David Mason)*

Preston Park was rebuilt ten years or so ago. This view looking north shows the carriage siding under the chalk cliffs, now covered in greenery. *(David Mason)*

Unit 7432 bring up the rear of the 17.35 to Victoria at Preston Park. (2/9/84) *(David Mason)*

The 17.48 to Brighton headed by Unit 7428 at Preston Park on 2nd September 1984. *(David Mason)*

Index